The Cutting Edge

To my parents, my husband Andrius and Asta Bangute – RA

The Cutting Edge

Innovation and Entrepreneurship in
New Europe

Edited by

Ruta Aidis

Honorary Senior Researcher, University College London, UK

and

Friederike Welter

*Professor, University of Siegen, Germany and TeliaSonera
Professor for Entrepreneurship, Stockholm School of
Economics in Riga, Latvia*

Edward Elgar
Cheltenham, UK • Northampton, MA, USA

Published by
Edward Elgar Publishing Limited
Glensanda House
Montpellier Parade
Cheltenham
Glos GL50 1UA
UK

Edward Elgar Publishing, Inc.
William Pratt House
9 Dewey Court
Northampton
Massachusetts 01060
USA

A catalogue record for this book
is available from the British Library

ISBN 978 1 84542 974 4

Printed and bound in Great Britain by MPG Books Ltd, Bodmin, Cornwall

Contents

Figures

Tables

Contributors

Ruta Aidis, University College London, UK

Kate Bishop, Imperial College London and Honorary Researcher, SSEES, University College London, UK

Kazimierz Kubiak, Chamber of Commerce in Zgierz, Poland

Tatiana S. Manolova, Bentley College, USA

Tõnis Mets, University of Tartu, Estonia

Lisa Papania, Simon Fraser University, Canada

Anna Rogut, University of Lódź and Academy of Management, Poland

Arnis Sauka, Stockholm School of Economics in Riga, Latvia

Daniel Shapiro, Simon Fraser University, Canada

Ágnes Tibor, Budapest Polytechnic, Hungary

Aleš Vahčič, University of Llubljana, Slovenia

Friederike Welter, University of Siegen, Germany and Stockholm School of Economics in Riga, Latvia

1. Introduction

Ruta Aidis and Friederike Welter

Currently, there is a dearth of information regarding innovative (and successful) enterprises in the countries that have most recently joined the European Union and which are often referred to as 'New Europe'. In the past, much emphasis has been placed on the barriers to entrepreneurship and innovation that exist in these countries. In this book, we shift the focus to the innovative potential that these environments provide and how entrepreneurs have been able to convert these possibilities into successful businesses. Through this collection of eight in-depth case studies, we illustrate how successful and innovative businesses were able to develop in each of these countries. The idea for such a book emerged from our research in Central and Eastern Europe and our interests in how enterprises developed during transition and after these countries joined the European Union. Both editors have come across fascinating stories showing the enormous adaptability of entrepreneurs in these countries that are often not reflected in statistical research. We hope that in sharing some of these stories with a wider audience this collection will contribute to deepening our understanding of what constitutes entrepreneurship and innovation in an enlarged Europe.

Each case study highlights specific aspects of the interplay between the institutional setting, the environment and the individual characteristics of the entrepreneur that created an 'enabling context' for innovative behaviour to develop and grow, drawing attention to the opportunities and constraints offered in each environment. Additionally, each case study presents an overview of the country's key economic indicators and the role of small and medium-sized enterprises (SMEs) in the economy.

Below we first briefly introduce the case studies contained in this book. This is followed by a summary discussion comparing the main themes raised in the individual case studies.

SUMMARY OF THE CASE STUDIES

In Chapter 2, Kate Bishop explores the role of the internal, external, strategic and network factors in the growth and development process of

Dekonta, a knowledge-based firm in the Czech republic. Dekonta was founded in 1992 by twin brothers, aged in their forties and with professional degrees and experience in engineering. It is a small firm established to pursue and commercialize a new technological invention in bioremediation and was the first *de novo* environmental service firm in the Czech Republic.

A crucial element for the establishment of Dekonta was government demand for environmental services, which continues to affect Dekonta's operations via the tendering process, regulations and promotion of R&D within the sector. In 1992 the government adopted a privatization strategy for industrial companies which involves the government taking responsibility for the remediation of these firms on a contract basis. This generated a lot of work in the field of remediation of contaminated soil. Thus the transition process, in particular the privatization programme, created a new market opportunity in environmental services which Dekonta has taken advantage of successfully.

In Chapter 3, Tatiana Manolova highlights the rise of the firm FILCOM/FILKAB in Bulgaria. This case, in particular, shows how hard work, realistic strategic objectives, persistence and a matter-of-fact approach to strategy execution provide a basis for distinct and durable competitive advantage in a transitional environment.

FILCOM was started in 1990 by four friends to fill the niche of trade in electrical equipment. In 1999 it was turned into a joint stock company and renamed FILKAB. In addition to distributing cables, wires and electrical equipment, it also provides engineering services and assembly of electrical parts. Even within Bulgaria's sometimes unclear legal environment, FILKAB demonstrated its integrity and commitment to business ethics by paying top wages, offering comprehensive health and retirement benefits and through strict compliance with labour and safety regulations. It also has a very democratic work environment with no secretaries or receptionists. As a result of these policies and practices, fewer than ten employees have left the company in its 16 years of existence. Furthermore it has won the 'taxpayer of the year' award three times. In essence, FILKAB chose the path of starting a legal business and 'following the rules' from its inception.

Chapter 4, written by Tõnis Mets, focuses on Estonia and the development of Regio. Rivo Noorkõiv was the CEO of Regio, which was founded as a small state-owned enterprise in the mid-1980s. But soon after Estonia issued a decree allowing for the existence of joint stock companies, Regio became a private company. It was first based at the University of Tallin. Regio's initial niche market for cartography was created by the Soviet Union's reluctance to provide accurate geographical data in the native language of its republics. Later it expanded its operations to mapping, geospatial data, geographical information systems, and mobile positioning.

The private firm began with two co-founders: Rivo and a geographer from the University of Tallin, Jüri Jagomägi. Juri also brought in his son Teet who at the time was 19 years of age. In order to improve their knowledge and use of technology, Teet was sent to the US for training as a programmer from 1992 to 1993. Upon returning to Regio, at the age of 23, Teet was appointed the company's CEO.

The technological advantage that Regio illustrates stems from the 'late-comer effect'. As Tõnis Mets argues, Regio was not restricted by old technological investments. The new modern knowledge obtained by Teet while in the US enabled Regio to start digital cartography from scratch because they were not limited by any old systems or practices. This enabled Regio to incorporate new ideas and technology more easily since there were no conflicts with any previous investments. In addition, the economic and social development processes in Estonia and its accession to the EU created more confidence in the domestic business environment.

This case also provides insights into the challenges of obtaining financing for business growth in the transitional context. For Regio, financing was finally secured through risk capital from the Baltics Small Equity Fund. It also exemplifies the difficulties of participating in an international merger. In the case of Regio, the merger did not last long. Ownership was taken back by Regio's initial founders after only a few years, when the new company went bankrupt.

In Hungary, even under the centrally-planned system, small businesses were able to operate, albeit in a limited way. Chapter 5 by Ágnes Tibor focuses on the new generation of entrepreneurs that emerged during transition in Hungary in the fledgling IT sector. These 'new' entrepreneurs, such as Márton Balog and his friend Dávid Szőts, tend to be young and creative, to like challenges and to be full of energy and business ideas. The embryonic idea for Prohardver emerged in 1998 when Márton and Dávid, both 19 years old, began to buy and sell computer parts. Their work was initially a hobby; they started testing computers and computer parts and made the test results publicly available on the internet 'just for fun'. At that time no one else was doing this in Hungary. As their popularity grew, they enjoyed their monopoly position. Having introduced something completely new to the market and having no direct competitors, Márton and Dávid were engaged in 'learning by doing'. Over time, and already being successful, Márton and Dávid decided to turn their hobby into a registered company in 2000. The main 'customers' (that is, visitors) to their site were producers and wholesalers, do-it-yourselfers and corporate buyers of IT products, while their main source of income was advertising. The case takes us up to the present, when Márton Balog is CEO at the age of 26 and considering how to diversify Prohardver into foreign markets.

In Chapter 6, Ruta Aidis focuses on Tomas Juška, the CEO of Libra Holding, in order to describe the development of the largest wood processing company in Lithuania. Tomas and his four friends started Libragroup in 1992. They were between 20 and 24 years of age and knew nothing about wood or wood processing, nor were they aware that the sector had any great potential. By 2006 Libra Group reorganized under the name Libra Holding, having grown to consist of 12 distinct companies exporting to 20 countries worldwide.

Libra Holding is striking in terms of its business philosophy and company strategy. As CEO, Tomas stresses the positive aspects of the transition environment when he emphasizes the great ambition that individuals in transition countries have to improve their livelihoods and the quality of life in their home country. If a company can harness this drive, then it can achieve tremendous success. In Tomas's view, Lithuanians have a deeper drive for achievement than in the old EU countries since they are trying to rebuild their native country to the level it was at fifty years ago, before the Soviet occupation. This philosophy has paid off in terms of attracting and retaining employees. Further, Libra Holding also maintains competitiveness by enhancing internal human capital resources in order to improve efficiency and productivity through its Libra School: a cultural centre which encourages, inspires and provides direction for further personal development of Libra Holding's employees. Finally, Libra Holding was able to cultivate the drive and patriotism of their employees to benefit its business activities and create a high level of team spirit and morale.

In Chapter 7, Arnis Sauka and Friederike Welter choose the case of Safety Ltd to illustrate how the specific transition context in Latvia influences the ability to convert new innovative opportunities into successful businesses. Safety Ltd was started by Peteris and two friends, Juris and Ivars, in 1994. Peteris and Juris had previous experience in setting up or working in private companies. Ivars had no business experience, but after losing his job as a tailor in one of the big Soviet factories, he was earning an income by working for himself sewing clothes. Though they had different backgrounds, they all shared the dream of getting rich. They decided to use Ivars's tailoring experience in order to start a business manufacturing men's suits. This business idea did not go exactly as planned.

By chance, Peteris came across a catalogue advertising uniforms for shop assistants in Germany – something that was still non-existent in Latvia! Initially no one seemed interested, since it necessitated a completely new way of thinking. But gradually they began receiving orders and are now a successfully established small company with 23 employees.

Entrepreneurship survived in Poland even during the centrally-planned period, but the nature of entrepreneurship changed during the transition process. Anna Rogut and Kazimierz Kubiak present the case of Mieczysław Kozera in Chapter 8. In 1981, at 30 years of age, Kozera lost his job after martial law was imposed in Poland. He had a technical background and experience and he applied that to his entrepreneurial endeavour. He borrowed a substantial amount of money from his brother and some family members to establish a store selling ceramic and glass products (artistic glass) and household appliances. There was a high demand for and low supply of these products in the initial transition stages, which aided the development of his company. In 1989 he was able to acquire a bankrupt rubber plant so that he could further expand his operations. He adapted the plant into a small glassware factory. Since he knew little about this field, he hired some experienced employees.

Kozera was astute to new market developments and noticed the rising demand for ceramic garden products in Poland as the standard of living continued to improve. He decided to buy one hectare of land in 1992 on which to build a ceramics factory. He was able to buy most of the equipment needed from bankrupt companies that had over-invested in their equipment. Kozera also diversified into unrelated areas such as petrol stations and a wholesale fuel delivery operation. His profits from fuel sales were reinvested in the development of furniture centres and another glassware manufacturing plant. He further diversified into the hotel service sector, building a hotel and also a shopping and service centre. In order to develop his staff, Kozera's company has its own training programme for technical and shop floor assistants. The owner is also planning on opening a Professional Training Centre in order to ensure the constant influx of qualified personnel.

In spite of its diverse operations, Kozera's company which is named after himself, remains a sole tradership and its organizational structure is very simple. Kozera himself is a one-man management board supervising the different operations. The influence of transition is clear in the case of Kozera. As Rogut and Kubiak argue, had he not been dimissed from work during martial law, Mr Kozera would probably still be an ordinary worker in a state-owned enterprise.

In Chapter 9, Daniel Shapiro, Aleš Vahčič and Lisa Papania showcase the development of Seaway in Slovenia. Slovenia was part of the communist system of Yugoslavia which had a fairly liberal view towards private business ownership, albeit with clear limitations. Seaway was founded in 1989 by two brothers, Japec and Jernej, and grew to be one of the world's leading developers of sailing boats and power boats, engaged in the end-to-end production process from design, engineering and tooling to the manufacture of components. It sells its products and services globally, and is currently the leading producer of rudders and bearings for sailing boats.

Its competitive advantage is, in part, based on its design and innovation capabilities, for which it has won numerous international awards, and which have enabled it to grow into a profitable mid-size producer of luxury boats.

The brothers came from an advantaged background. Both were highly educated: Jernej was an architect and worked for a period in Germany (gaining foreign experience and contacts) and Japec was a medical doctor and a cardiology researcher. Seaway developed out of a shared hobby as amateur yacht builders. In the 1980s amateur yacht building was a popular hobby amongst the Slovene elite who sought to imitate a Western lifestyle. As professionals and academics, Japec and Jernej were outside the ruling networks of the day, which may have played to their entrepreneurial advantage. Individuals embedded in the ruling networks tend to be more focused on developing existing ventures more closely linked to the political elite. However it also meant that their opportunity costs were high as they were both professionals seeking a risky career change.

In 2000 it became apparent that future growth would require the company to move beyond design to manufacturing its own moulds and tools with robotic technology. However, Seaway generated insufficient funds internally to buy this technology and needed outside financing. They sought and received venture capitalist investment but this led to the dilution of control and pressures to install professional management. This case clearly illustrates not only the critical importance of venture capital and financial markets in the process of growth for an innovative firm but also its conflicts.

ENTREPRENEURSHIP AND INNOVATION IN 'NEW EUROPE': ISSUES EMERGING FROM THE CASES

Taken together the stories of the entrepreneurs featured in the case studies provide insights into some of the typical features that characterize entrepreneurship in transition countries as well as illustrating some of the differences. As these eight case studies show, tolerance of entrepreneurs and small businesses during the centrally-planned period varied. Some forms of entrepreneurship existed in Poland, Hungary and Slovenia even during the centrally-planned period but entrepreneurship was severely restricted in Bulgaria, Czechoslovakia and the three Baltic States that had been part of the Soviet Union (Estonia, Latvia and Lithuania). But even in the countries where entrepreneurship of some kind was permitted, it was fundamentally different in nature, given the constraints of the centrally-planned system.

With the advent of transition, private enterprises became legal. But central planning has left an unfavourable legacy in the tendency of the general population to harbour negative attitudes towards these new entrepreneurs. While some of the early free-market entrepreneurs may have deserved this, other entrepreneurs trying to set up viable, honest enterprises, also had to contend with these negative attitudes. Consequently, one of the characteristics that many of the entrepreneurs discussed in this book share is an ability to persevere in a turbulent environment under adverse conditions.

Given the novelty of the private enterprise sector in these countries, it is not surprising that most of the enterprises were started from scratch, an experience common to all the transition countries. Only one enterprise, namely Regio in Estonia, grew out of a state-owned enterprise. This trend also might be seen as an indicator for the entrepreneurial drive that individuals in these countries showed once private entrepreneurship was allowed. This is partly reflected in the motives for entering entrepreneurship. The reasons given by the business founders for starting their businesses provide insights into the push as well as the pull mechanisms that exist in the transitional landscape. The Polish case (Kozera) illustrates the classic situation of an individual pushed into entrepreneurship after losing his job in a state-owned enterprise. Many individuals lost their jobs due to downsizing and the closure of state-owned enterprises. With no other means of support, these individuals often started their own enterprises as a way to make ends meet. In the case of Kozera, necessity-driven entrepreneurship opened up a tremendous opportunity that resulted in an extremely successful venture, thus pointing out the learning curves of entrepreneurs. Most of the other cases illustrate the various pull mechanisms operating in the transitional setting. Prohardver in Hungary and Seaway in Slovenia illustrate how individuals with limited experience or background turn a hobby into a successful business. Libra Holding in Lithuania was started by students who viewed their business start-up as if it were all 'a bit of a game', while the founders of Safety Ltd were motivated by the 'universal' 'pull' motive of 'wanting to get rich'. Other cases, such as Dekonta in the Czech Republic, illustrate individuals taking advantage of an opportunity that was created during transition.

In general the eight enterprises showcased in this book were set up by entrepreneurial teams made up of friends (Safety Ltd and Libra Holding) and friendly neighbours (Filkab), but also by brothers (Dekonta and Seaway) and pairs of friends (Prohardver) and colleagues (Regio). This might reflect the importance of pooling resources in a transition environment, which in the case of starting a new venture is best done by teaming up with partners. It may also indicate the importance of creating an internal support structure, which in most cases was severely lacking in the transitional environment, via co-founders. Only one case study was set up by an individual (Kozera) who remained a sole proprietor even during the firm's growth and expansion. Most entrepreneurs were individuals with professional experience (Dekonta, Filkab, Regio, Safety Ltd, Kozera and Seaway). However in two cases, the entrepreneurs were students with no formal work experience (Prohardver and Libra Holding). All of these successful enterprises were started in the early stage of the transition process (1980s or early 1990s, depending on the country). As is typical in transition countries, most of the entrepreneurs presented in these case studies are young, university educated and male.

The challenges encountered by the entrepreneurs in these eight transition countries also capture the way in which, in spite of the obstacles, it is possible to be successful in a turbulent environment. One such 'turbulence' is caused by weak institutions that allow for corruption, informal networks and the prevalence of bribery in influencing private business development. In addition, most of these business owners had to contend with an environment where outside funding for start-up or business growth was in most cases non-existent. Given these barriers, it is interesting to observe the range of strategies these eight successful firms have used to address them. In terms of interference, not all firms seemed to notice it, either because it is a pervasive element in the environment and it is something the entrepreneurs have simply learned to 'deal with' or because the firms seemed to be 'off the radar' of rent-seeking officials because of the inexperience and youth of the entrepreneurs and the relative unattractiveness of the chosen industry (Libra Holding). Some firms, such as Filkab, have chosen to uphold their commitment to business ethics. However for others, the corrupt environment remains a barrier and may even influence the decision to cease operations in the future (Safety Ltd).

Even though the transition process was a source of many challenges for these entrepreneurs, especially in the early stages of transition in terms of the weak institutional environment, instability of regulation, excessive governmental interference, corruption and so on, it also provided tremendous opportunities for innovation, business development and growth that are unparalleled in mature market economies. Some opportunities arose as a result of government demand for specific activities, such as the need for waste management through bioremediation (Dekonta), or in areas previously restricted and controlled by the government, such as map making and global positioning (Regio). But mostly, opportunities resulted from the entrepreneurs taking the risk to enter previously under-developed and/or neglected sectors such as quality uniforms (Safety Ltd), wood processing (Libra Holding), electrical equipment (Filkab), ceramics and glass products (Kozera) and luxury yachts (Seaway). In addition, new technological developments created opportunities to grow in previously non-existent sectors (Prohardver).

The financial constraints for private sector development in transition countries are well-documented in the literature. In order to succeed, most of the entrepreneurs in these case studies had to develop strategies to address this barrier that are typical for the transitional environment. Some were able to borrow start-up capital from friends and/or relatives (Safety Ltd and Kozera), while others used capital obtained through an earlier business (Libra Holding). In one case (Prohardver), the founders chose initially to operate on a shoestring budget as a strategy to start a business without access to external financing. Financing future growth is another issue that a number of enterprises needed to address. Some companies, such as Kozera and Libra Holding, were able to finance their growth through reinvesting their profits, while Regio and Seaway needed to finance rapid expansion through external financing, which proved very difficult to obtain and often created additional problems.

In addition to providing tremendous opportunities for business development, the transition environment provided additional benefits that have led to the successful development of the eight companies highlighted in these case studies. All the case studies recognize the important and positive role in their business development played by human capital in the form of education inherited from the former centrally-planned system. Two case studies (Regio and Libra Holding) also stress the advantage of harnessing the power of patriotism and pride and the desire of individuals to catch up with the West in rebuilding their countries as free market economies as a very important incentive to operating in the transition context.

The experience of starting and growing a successful business in the turbulent transition environment also offers unique opportunities for further business expansion in other transition countries (Dekonta, Kozera, Safety Ltd, Libra Holding) or developing countries (Regio), thus indicating possibly differing internationalization patterns of new firms originating in a transition context.

All eight case studies highlight the forms of innovation that have taken place in the transition country environment. Most commonly, innovation in transition countries occurs through the introduction of a product known in Western economies but absolutely new to the developing domestic market (Safety Ltd, Filkab, Prohardver, Libra Holding and Kozera). Here, innovation is the result of taking the risk of introducing a completely new product or service into a turbulent ever-changing environment. In many cases, these entrepreneurs had to be forward-looking risk-takers, predicting the demand that would develop for their products. More typical forms of innovation, also characteristic of mature Western countries, include new sector development such as that illustrated by Dekonta in the area of bioremediation. In order to develop the most competitive designs, Seaway used the strategy of consulting lead users to introduce innovations to an existing sector. The lack of modern technology inadvertently allowed Regio to take advantage of the 'latecomer effect' by applying the latest new technologies to the development of innovative new products competitive on international markets.

'Learning by doing' can be seen as a form of innovation especially relevant in the turbulent environments that characterize early transition. In all of our cases, previously neglected areas of products and services were introduced into the domestic economy for profit. Though in many cases, the product or service already existed in another mature economy, it had not previously existed in the transition country. Transition adds an additional dimension to an entrepreneur's risk in starting a new business: macroeconomic instability and the uncertainty of demand coupled with an ever-changing regulatory environment.

To conclude, the cases reported in this book illustrate the variety of development paths taken by enterprises in economies where some entrepreneurship was tolerated throughout Soviet times (for example, Poland or Hungary) and those countries where no private entrepreneurship was allowed (for example, Bulgaria, the Baltic States, Czech and Slovak Republics). However, the case studies also demonstrate a need – both for researchers and policymakers – to take into account the specifics of not only the country environment, but also the transition process and its impact on entrepreneurship development and innovation, if entrepreneurship is to be analysed correctly and support measures are to be targeted in such a way that these innovative firms can contribute to economic development.

2. Dekonta: a post-Velvet Revolution fairy tale of diversification and internationalization

Kate Bishop

INTRODUCTION

This chapter describes the growth and development of a knowledge-based entrepreneurial venture, Dekonta a.s.,[1] one of the leading waste management, consulting and engineering companies in the Czech Republic. The Czech Republic makes for an interesting back drop to the case study: after the Velvet Revolution in Czechoslovakia in November 1989 and the subsequent separation into two republics in 1993, Czechoslovakia underwent fundamental economic and political reform to become a democratic, stable, market-oriented economy. Under the previous centrally-planned system entrepreneurship had been severely restricted; therefore one of the key policy tasks was to create the incentives and conditions conducive to private sector development. Despite suffering from two recessions caused by the initiation of the transition process and the Velvet Revolution, the small and medium-sized enterprise (SME) sector has grown and the share of organizations with 50 to 249 employees increased from 21.2 per cent in 1994 to almost 25 per cent in 2000 (UNIDO 2001). However compared to other EU countries the number of SMEs is relatively low as several barriers to private sector development persist, namely poor availability of finance and burdensome tax regulation.

The issue of knowledge-based entrepreneurship is becoming more and more important in both advanced Western European countries and for the new member states of the EU as it offers a number of opportunities. For example, it can multiply the channels by which scientific knowledge is transferred to commercial application, attract additional scientifically educated human capital into the process of adapting new theoretical and procedural knowledge to practical applications, and create new employment opportunities in newly emerging small businesses that may have growth potential.

This is especially important given the relaunching of the Lisbon Strategy in

March 2005 with its renewed focus on growth, innovation and employment.[2] Meeting the Lisbon objectives will be partly determined by the ability of new member states to restructure towards knowledge-based activities. The Czech Republic is taking the Lisbon Agenda seriously and recognizes that this can play a role in the country's economic development and competitiveness. As a result a number of policy objectives on research and development (R&D), innovation and SME development have been established.

I will use the case of Dekonta, a knowledge-based venture, to answer the following two key questions:

1. What is the role of the 'enabling environment' or internal, external, strategic and network factors in the growth and development process of this knowledge-based firm within the transition context?
2. How does the role of these factors change over time?

This chapter aims to describe the key factors behind the growth and development process, in particular the role of human capital, relationships, strategy and institutions. It adopts an 'enabling context' view of the firm and examines the role of internal, strategic, network and external factors in the firm's development process. Dekonta is a small firm, only thirteen years old, involved in a strategic sector. It was established to pursue and commercialize a new technological invention in bioremediation[3] and provides an excellent subject for exploring our key questions.[4]

The concept of knowledge-based entrepreneurship has been widely debated (Grant 1996; Nonaka 1994), but for the purposes of this chapter knowledge-based entrepreneurship refers to the transmission of knowledge that has been generated within the fields of science and technology in anticipation of commercial application. In particular the emphasis is on the development of new technologies, the introduction of new products and processes, and on the actors, including new firms, universities and sources of external finance. Dekonta meets this definition of a knowledge-based venture.

First, the economic and demographic situation, and the details of innovation performance and the waste management sector in the Czech Republic are presented, followed by a detailed discussion of the development of Dekonta within the Czech Republic.

OPPORTUNITIES AND CONSTRAINTS FOR ENTREPRENEURS IN THE CZECH REPUBLIC

The Czech Republic has a relatively strong economic position compared to some of the other transition countries in terms of several macroeconomic

*Table 2.1   Economic and demographic situation in selected transition
          countries*

	Czech Republic	Slovak Republic	Hungary	Poland
Population in millions	10.2	5.4	10.1	38.2
Area ('000 sq.km)	78.9	49	93	313.9
GDP (in billion US$ 2004)	107	41.1	100.3	241.8
GDP per capita in 2004 at current international US$ PPP[a]	19 311	14 549	16 596	12 876
Private sector share in GDP in 2005 (%)	80	80	80	75
Inflation 2005 estimation (%)	2	2.4	3.8	2.2
Unemployment rate in 2003 (%)	7.8	17.1	5.8	19.2
FDI inflows 2004 (as % of GDP)	3.7	1	3.6	2
Est. level of real GDP in 2004	114	121	120	142

Note: a. This is a method of measuring the relative purchasing power of different
countries' currencies over the same types of goods and services.

Source: EBRD (2005); UNECE (2006).

fundamentals. As Table 2.1 shows it has achieved a high percentage of the private sector's share of GDP, and enjoys a strong GDP per capita position. It also has one of the lowest inflation rates and has managed to overcome its unemployment problem, with an unemployment rate of just 7.8 per cent in 2003, which is quite low compared to some other countries of the region, particularly Poland and the Slovak Republic.

Table 2.2 presents several indicators on the ease of doing business in the transition region. It appears that the Czech Republic suffers from quite burdensome labour regulations (hiring and firing costs) relative to other East European countries, such as Poland. However, with regard to starting a business in terms of per capita income, the Czech Republic is not as costly as the overall regional level (8.9 per cent compared to 14.1 per cent for the region as a whole). Dealing with licences does not appear to be too problematic either in the Czech Republic, compared to many of the other transition countries.

Table 2.3 reports the share of employees in all SMEs compared to the total number of employees in the economy as a whole. It illustrates that the Czech Republic has a slightly lower share of employees in SMEs (albeit an increasing share) compared to several other transition economies.

Svejnar (1995) details the economic background of the Czech Republic which exhibited several advantageous building blocks for the economic

Table 2.2   The business environment in selected transition countries

	Czech Republic	Slovak Republic	Hungary	Poland	Region
Starting a business (% per capita income)	8.9	4.8	20.9	21.4	14.1
Dealing with licences (% per capita income)	14.5	17.1	260	85.6	564.9
Hiring workers (% salary)	35	35.2	35.2	21.4	26.7
Firing costs (weeks of wages)	21.7	13	34.5	13	26.2
Registering property (% property value)	3	0.1	11	2	2.7
Public credit registry coverage (% adults)	3.5	1	0	0	1.7
Total tax rate (% profit)	49	48.9	59.3	38.4	56
Enforcing a contract (% debt)	14.1	15.7	9.6	10	15
Closing a business (% estate)	14.5	18	14.5	22	14.3

Source: World Bank Doing Business Indicators.

Table 2.3   Share of SME sector in employment in selected transition countries

Percentage of SME employees as compared to the total number of employees in the economy as a whole	2002	2003
Czech Republic	56	57
Hungary	57	n.a.
Slovakia	62	66
Poland	68	n.a.

Source: UNECE (2005).

reforms which began in 1989. Firstly, in the 1930s Czechoslovakia was ranked among the 10 major European industrial countries and possessed a large number of skilled craftsmen and businessmen proficient at exporting goods. This allowed the roots of entrepreneurship to take hold in society. It also made it easier for reformers in the 1990s to push through radical policies, as the majority of the population were keen to once again reinstate themselves as an advanced European country. Furthermore the communist system left behind a legacy of strong human capital, as emphasis had been placed on universal primary education, general and technical secondary education. This strong human capital base has been an asset for the transition process in general as well as at the individual level in terms of innovation capabilities.

However on the eve of transition, the remnants of the communist regime also posed a number of difficulties for economic reformers, especially in terms of the extreme degree of state control which had resulted in a virtually complete government ownership of the economy and a dearth of private business due to the severe restriction of entrepreneurship in the centrally-planned era. In contrast, the communist governments tolerated entrepreneurial activity in Poland and Hungary.[5] Czechoslovakia was also much more integrated into the Soviet bloc's economic structure than were Poland and Hungary, which made it more vulnerable to the collapse of the CMEA (Council for Mutual Economic Assistance) trade bloc.

Following the Velvet Revolution in 1989–90, state policy was concerned with creating an environment conducive to the development of an SME sector, which is considered a crucial part of the transition process (McDermott 1991). A study conducted by the Rhine Westphalia Institute for Economic Research and published by the OECD (1996) documents how the method of mass privatization in Czechoslovakia helped develop the private sector and contribute to industrial production.

Bohatá and Mládek (1999) describe the operation of the Entrepreneurial Law of April 1990, which legalized the establishment of private companies. The privatization process (1990–93) consisted of large and small scale[6] privatization (along with restitution) which helped contribute to the creation of a private sector in retail trade, wholesale trade and services. They also note how a well-functioning infrastructure to assist SMEs needed to be installed. As a lack of outside financing was a major barrier for SMEs in the Czech Republic, one of the first steps was to set up the Czech Moravian Guarantee Development Bank (CMZRB), which was established in 1992 to provide guarantees on operation credits, financial assistance to repay credits and consultancy. This assistance was carried out via programmes such as START to assist start ups and ZARUKA, which provided collateral for SMEs.

Yet constraints to entrepreneurial development still exist. A recent survey of entrepreneurs in the Czech Republic by Ernst and Young (2006) revealed that the economic transition process has created several problems for the SME sector. The respondents mentioned that the Czech tax system suffers from two weaknesses: insufficient transparency and frequent changes to regulations. Also the majority of respondents agreed that the formal requirements related to the employment and retention of staff constitute the biggest burden for Czech entrepreneurs. Moreover, nearly all of the entrepreneurs interviewed had to rely on their own sources of financing and commented that the poor availability of finance was a serious issue, highlighting the fact that much still needs to be done in the sphere of financial assistance for entrepreneurs.

INNOVATION AND THE KNOWLEDGE-BASED ECONOMY IN THE CZECH REPUBLIC

The new Innovation Policy for 2005–10 was developed by the Deputy Prime Minister for the Economy and the Ministry of Education and Industry and Trade, in light of the recommendations of the European Council Presidency. It has four strategic objectives: (1) strengthening R&D as a source of innovation; (2) establishing a working private–public partnership; (3) securing human resources for innovation; and (4) improving the public sector's research, development and innovation performance. The policy sets out various tasks in order to meet these objectives. For example, in order to strengthen R&D as a source of innovation, a target has been set to increase public expenditure each year and attain the level of 1 per cent of GDP by 2010, with a particular focus on industrial research. Also efforts have been made to set long-term directions for research activities, as in the past there has been no attempt to tailor programmes. Furthermore, in order to salvage the Czech Republic's lagging performance in patent activity (Table 2.4) there will be a promotion of knowledge protection. For example, intellectual property rights (IPR) will be supported by a financial contribution from the state budget via a short-term financing scheme and IPR will begin to be taught in university programmes. In terms of business expenditure on R&D as a percentage of GDP, Table 2.4 shows that the Czech Republic is doing relatively well compared to its Eastern European counterparts such as Hungary, Poland and Slovakia.

The Czech Republic lags behind the EU15 in the number of science and engineering graduates (Table 2.4) and there is an impetus to increase human resources for innovation activities. Currently there is an attempt to match the demand trends of the labour market with the development of relevant university programmes. Table 2.4 also shows that the Czech Republic is performing well in terms of employment in medium to high-tech manufacturing, and is currently reaching levels above that of the EU15.

Several developments in the policy arena which have impacted upon innovation activities within the waste management sector are pertinent for

Table 2.4　Knowledge creation and human resources in R&D in selected transition countries, 2003

	Czech Republic	Hungary	Poland	Slovakia	EU15
Public R&D expenditures (as % of GDP)	0.5	0.62	0.43	0.24	0.69
Business expenditure on R&D (% of GDP)	0.77	0.36	0.16	0.23	1.3
EPO[a] high-tech patent applications	10.9[a]	18.3[a]	2.7[a]	4.3[a]	31.6
New engineering and science graduates	5.6	3.7	8.3	7.4	11.3
Employment in med–high-tech manufacturing	8.94	8.5	4.35	8.21	7.41

Note:　a. European Patent Office; figures are for 2002.

Source:　European Commission (2003).

our case study. For example, in the run-up to EU accession, the Czech Republic took part in several programmes to meet EU environmental regulations and spent more than 2 per cent of GDP[7] on environmental issues. As the Czech economy is located on the 'black triangle'[8] and has been based on heavy industry, coal mining, steel and chemicals there is a strong demand for remediation and waste management services.

Demand thus far for these environmental services comes from the Environmental State Fund and the private sector, especially the energy and chemical sectors. This demand is being created by a number of new regulations and directives, for example, the EU Urban Wastewater Treatment Directive. A report by the Regional Environmental Centre for Central and Eastern Europe (REC 1997) noted that these new directives and the industrial background of the Czech Republic have created demand for a variety of specific environmental technologies. The report highlights the fact that there is enhanced scope for enterprises to become more receptive to innovative technologies as the enforcement of legislation improves and the cost of waste disposal grows, creating a possible niche for waste minimization technologies.

Overall, it appears that the waste management sector is becoming a high-tech sector within the Czech Republic. Moreover the sector is creating a number of new patents, such as a new method for drying biomass using air extraction devices (Brummack and Polster 2006).

DEKONTA A.S.: BACKGROUND, STRUCTURE, SERVICES AND INNOVATIVE POTENTIAL

Dekonta a.s. was founded in 1992 by twin brothers Petr and Pavel Mothejl along with a colleague Tomăš Havlik, all of whom are still involved in the day-to-day running of the firm. Petr and Pavel are in their early forties with similar backgrounds, both having studied at the faculty of building construction at the Czech Technical University. They both have masters' degrees in Engineering and work experience in leading environmental engineering firms such as EKOL spol. s.r.o. which specializes in steam and gas turbine operation. Tomăš Havlik, who is also in his forties, was educated in the field of chemistry and has extensive experience in bioremediation projects, although his role at Dekonta focuses on company strategy. The three of them used private savings to establish the firm. The motivation for establishing the firm came from Pavel who decided to introduce new bioremediation technologies to the Czech Republic after his experiences working in the field within the Russian market. For the first five years the focus was on these bioremediation techniques, but a change in strategy led to a whole package of technologies being offered.

Today, Dekonta is one of the leading waste management, consulting and engineering firms in the Czech Republic (these services are described in Table 2.6 below). The majority of the staff work in the headquarters and laboratories (while the subsidiaries employ a handful of people[9]). The subsidiaries deal with environmental consulting, landfill activities, risk assessment and water treatment.

In 2006 the firm employed approximately 150 staff from many different Central and Eastern European countries, including Poland, Slovakia and Romania. Table 2.5 shows the extent to which employment has grown since 1998. Dekonta's personnel have backgrounds in project management, lab and field work, engineering, biochemistry, geochemistry and biology; approximately half of them hold university degrees. Currently, Dekonta is entering a period of stability, following a big recruitment drive in 2004, owing to growth in international projects.

The main activities of Dekonta are based at Ústi nad Labem,[10] which is also the location of their waste incinerator, while their headquarters are located in Prague. There are also regional offices in Ostrava, Caslav, Brno and Dretovice, and technological centres in Slany, Ostrava and Ústi nad Labem. Dekonta has three daughter companies in the Czech Republic: AVAK Dekonta a.s., Biodegradace s.r.o. and Evo Služby. These companies are involved in the monitoring and development of sewage systems, water treatment, waste removal, remediation of soil and water, laboratory research and incineration. In addition Biodegradace s.r.o. provides an

Table 2.5   Summary table for Dekonta

	1998	2001	2004
Employees	20	71	137
Turnover in millions (euros)	3	6.5	22
Profit/loss (euros)	n.a.	–150 327	1 833 896
Education of core employees	50% of staff have university degrees, 30% are technicians, and 20% administrative workers. Many have backgrounds in biochemistry, geochemistry, geology and have previous industrial experience		
Core technologies	Bioremediation, bioventing, stabilization of soil/waste, bio-filtering		
Clients	Czech Ministry of Industry and Trade, Czech National Property Fund, World Bank, NATO, Lukoil, Skoda Plsen		

Table 2.6   Dekonta's services

Areas	Services
Waste management	Disposal of contaminated materials from hospitals and industrial sites, plus laboratory analyses and evaluation. Ústi nad Labem: the location of Dekonta's landfill, which is one of the largest waste incinerators.
Remediation of contaminated sites	Ex situ and in situ techniques for remediation of contaminated soil, sludge and ground water. Dekonta has experience of investigating, sampling and environmental monitoring of soil and bedrock, waste sediment, ground and surface water and soil air.
Laboratory services and research	Labs are equipped to carry out tests on the biodegradation of the contaminated soils, anaerobic and aerobic biological treatment of contaminated waters.
Consultancy services	Consultancy in environmental protection, due diligence, environmental impact assessment and noise studies.
Environmental emergency response	Services range from eliminating the contaminant to the complete recovery of a site.

accident and emergency response service. The company has also developed a number of joint ventures with Russian, Turkish and Hungarian firms[11] and has subsidiaries in Serbia and Montenegro, Slovakia, Poland and Romania. Table 2.6 illustrates the variety of services offered by Dekonta.

INNOVATION POTENTIAL AND GROWTH PATHS

Dekonta is continuously developing new technologies. In 2005 two patents were filed: a new separation process of heterogeneous material mixtures and a purification process of soil extracts containing polychlorinated biphenyls and anion active wetting agents. Furthermore, Petr Mothejl has been heavily involved in the delivery of environmental technologies such as the practical testing for atmogeochemical[12] plants and the development of technology for transporting oil sludge.

Dekonta is unique in its area as it is one of the first *de novo* environmental services firms in the Czech Republic. Dekonta differentiates itself from competitors by its diversity of operations, which include an emergency response service that is fully integrated into the National Emergency Response Team, incineration and laboratory facilities, along with a portfolio of remediation technologies. Also Dekonta's organizational flexibility distinguishes it from competitors such as Earth Tech and Aquatest, which facilitates its reaction to the needs of the market.

The management team at Dekonta made a strategic decision in the late 1990s to internationalize gradually as illustrated by their decision to serve foreign markets and progressively open subsidiaries in Poland, the Slovak Republic, Serbia and Montenegro, and Romania. Moreover, they have recently expanded their international operations by creating a joint venture in Turkey. Dekonta has been motivated to internationalize for two main reasons. First, as a result of domestic market decline due to the market saturation for some of its services, and second, in order to exploit certain core competences that lie in their knowledge of their East European neighbours.

THE ROLE OF THE ENABLING ENVIRONMENT AT DEKONTA

In this section we examine the role of the 'enabling environment' on the growth and development of Dekonta. First we explore the internal environment followed by a discussion of the importance of relationships for Dekonta. We conclude with a presentation of the external factors that have contributed to Dekonta's success.

Internal Environment: Skills, Vision, Innovation and Strategy Effects on Growth

At Dekonta, internal resources are vital to the growth and development process, as shown in Table 2.7. Both entrepreneurial vision and the skills of

Table 2.7   Assessment of the determinants of growth from the internal environment[a]

Dekonta's determinants of growth	1992	2006
Skills of employees	4	4
Entrepreneurial vision	4	3
Innovation efforts	3	3
Strategy: decision to internationalize	1	3

Note: a. These factors are measured on a 1–5 Likert scale, with 1 being the least important, to 5 being the most important. The scores are based an average ranking of responses to the following question: 'What is the importance of the following factors influencing the growth and development of your firm?'

Source: Own survey.

its employees are ranked as the most important growth factor from the internal environment. Innovation efforts are ranked in the intermediate position, both currently and in 1992. The focus on entrepreneurial vision and skills is reflected in the combination of entrepreneurial, management and industrial experience which the general director (Karel Petrželka) and managing director (Robert Raschman) possess, along with the qualifications of core employees. Approximately half of the core employees hold university degrees, some specialized in geochemistry and hydrogeology. In general, the core employees spoke very highly of the managerial capabilities of the founders and top management team. Some quotes illustrate the ability of the management to implement a working environment and strong firm culture that are conducive to growth and innovativeness: 'The Directors are good at creating teams, they have good management techniques and they are all very professional' (Cristina Lupu, Environmental Engineer).

For example, the top management creates an effective team working atmosphere by arranging weekend activities such as skiing trips, in order to help strengthen team spirit. Martin Polak, a hydrogeologist at Dekonta emphasizes the benefits of this: 'Our strong team culture is a source of our competitive advantage.'

Others suggested that a source of Dekonta's competitive advantage lies with the professionalism and reliability of the core employees. Ondrej Urban, a project manager at Dekonta stressed the advantages of Dekonta's flexibility: 'Dekonta is very flexible, it reacts easily to needs of the market, a great advantage compared to some other similar private firms. A lot of the other firms were established pre-1989, so their structure is quite old and inflexible; it's hard for them to react quickly.'

One remnant of the centrally-planned system is the hierarchical structure of organizations, and as many of Dekonta's rivals date back to this period, some of them are suffering from over bureaucratization in the decision-making process. Although in terms of human and financial capital Dekonta is in a weaker position than some of its rivals, it has been able to increase its market share by responding quickly to the needs of clients.

Dekonta's strategy has become increasingly important over the life of the firm. Ondrej Urban, a project manager at Dekonta, mentioned that a diversification strategy had been used as a means of survival, as the volume of work stemming from the Czech Republic is likely to decline. This is related to the transition process and the ensuing decline in domestic demand, as mentioned by Lynn (1998) and Aidis (2005). During the first five years of operation, Dekonta focused on bioremediation but now a whole package of various technologies are being offered. At first they concentrated on biotechnology of contaminated soil, but slowly Dekonta has started to change the direction of its development, diversifying towards a wide range of physical and chemical services. They have also constructed a bio-filter for contaminated air and water. As Ondrej Urban further commented: 'We have diversified into other activities so we can survive . . . these support our main activities (site remediation).'

A similar motivation lies behind their decision to internationalize further. Since 2000, Dekonta has pursued an internationalization strategy, which is reflected in Table 2.7, showing that the role of internationalization has increased over time. They have decided to focus on Eastern operations as they believe they have an advantage in terms of location and language abilities, for instance many of the Dekonta personnel speak Russian and they have obvious advantages in terms of being familiar with the geographic territory. Moreover, Marie Komárková, a project manager, noted that attempting to internationalize into Western markets would be fraught with difficulties due to a lack of finance, networks and the existing high level of market saturation.

One example of this strategy has been the firm's decision to open a new subsidiary in Turkey with a Turkish partner named Engineering and Consultancy Ltd[13] (ELC), which owns the biggest landfill site in Turkey. This offers great potential in terms of clients and it is anticipated that it will represent a 'gateway to Asia' for Dekonta. Furthermore, Dekonta is also looking directly to countries in Asia for new projects, for example, a project began preparation in Vietnam in 2006, dealing with Dioxin, a dangerous chemical left by US soldiers during the Vietnam war.[14] The project includes educating the population about water and agriculture as well as the removal of Dioxin via incinerators fitted with a special dioxin filter.

The benefits of internationalization were highlighted by some of Dekonta's employees. Cristina Lupu noted: 'From international collaboration we learn new legislation and new experiences for example, from our Serbian and Montenegro partner.'

In particular, the strategic decision to internationalize has been beneficial in terms of innovative activities. By using ELC as a partner to enter the Turkish market Dekonta has gained access to complementary technologies in the field of geosynthetic design and application as well as landfill planning. Since Dekonta has recently diversified into landfill activities the acquisition of new skills and technologies related to this field are likely to play a positive role in its growth process. Diversification away from traditional biotechnology to more chemical and physical services (for example, water treatment) has opened up a new range of cheaper methods for Dekonta, which is becoming a source of competitive advantage for the firm.

Relationships: Motivations, Entry Modes and Consequences for Firm Growth

Relationships now play a very important role in the growth and development process of Dekonta. Furthermore, both the quality and quantity of relationships have increased in relevance for the growth of Dekonta over time. Anecdotal evidence illustrates how relationships have helped Dekonta pursue its internationalization strategy. Collaboration with competitors has been beneficial for Dekonta. As Cristina Lupu notes: 'Dekonta reacts to new problems with other firms . . . We collaborate with competitors with good results.'

Existing literature in the field of networks in transition economies include Grabher and Stark (1997) who use case studies from Hungary to illustrate the nature and origin of networks in the transition process. They find that business networks can be a crucial element of business modernization. In the case of the Czech Republic, Uhlíř (1998) illustrates how both pre- and post-communist networks can help the restructuring of firms and consequently the economic development of regions.

In this context Jan Patka, a project manager, noted that one of Dekonta's competitors, Earth Tech, uses Dekonta for contaminated soil projects, due to their strong reputation in this field. The top management team, made up of Robert Raschman and Karel Petrželka, also emphasized how relationships with other firms were vital to the growth of Dekonta: 'We use other firms' methods: we learn from their losses or wins . . . we are in a small country we have to be friends with everybody, it's a necessity!' (Karel Petrželka). Robert Raschman, the managing director, further stressed: 'Relationships are crucial in our growth and development process.'

As for the rationale for building relationships, some of the most frequent responses from Robert and Karel highlighted the importance of exchanging information and bidding for joint projects. Concerning building relationships with foreign firms the main motivation is to obtain information about the local market and gain a locational advantage. These findings support the work of Baum et al. (2000) who find that relationships can provide contact with social, technological and commercial sources of competitive advantage. Interestingly, Dekonta has developed these relationships through personal networks acquired during previous work experience or from university contacts.

It is apparent that relationships have also figured in Dekonta's decision to internationalize. Dekonta's partnership with ELC in Turkey provides an opportunity to gain knowledge of the local market and access to new technologies. This supports the work of Coviello and Munro (1997) who find that a successful internationalization process depends on firms' involvement in international networks with partners guiding market entry and selection.

External Influences: The Role of Demand and the Political Environment in the Growth Process

Begley et al. (2005) and Van de Ven (1994) argue that government regulation and institutional arrangements can either facilitate or hinder the emergence of new technologies and industries. In this context, Table 2.8 illustrates how the role of the political and legal situation is crucial for Dekonta. The interviews revealed that the government was responsible for

Table 2.8   The changing role of the external environment[a]

	Dekonta's perception of the external environment	
	1992	2006
Government: political/legal environment	4	4
Demand (domestic)	5	4
Demand (foreign)	1	4

Note: a. These factors are measured on a 1–5 Likert scale, with 1 being the least important and 5 being the most important. The scores are based on an average ranking of responses to the question: 'How would you assess the role of the external environment in the growth and development of the business?'

Source: Own survey.

creating the initial demand for environmental services and it still has an impact on Dekonta's operations via the tendering process, regulations and promotion of R&D within the sector.

As Robert Raschman, the managing director, notes, 'In 1992 the Government adopted the strategy that industrial companies will be privatized and that the Government will take responsibility for the remediation of these firms, on a contract basis. This [decision] generated 1–2 billion euros worth of business and helped form environmental services firms. This created a lot of work in the field of remediation of contaminated soil. New activities in environmental services were needed, and it was the Government who created this demand.'

Thus it appears that the transition process, in particular the privatization programme has created a new market opportunity in environmental services, which Dekonta has successfully exploited.

The government is also active in encouraging R&D and Dekonta has already had five R&D projects funded by the Czech Ministry of Finance, Trade and Industry. However government policy has also created some hindrances for Dekonta, mainly through the implementation of bureaucratic regulation. As Ondrej Urban, a project manager points out: 'The State can be stubborn and not open to new things. We have developed a new technology for contaminated soil, but we are not sure we are able to operate this technology. It's a long approval process to get permission and persuade them. The state is a key player.'

In the past Dekonta has suffered from the effects of corruption, especially in the business tendering process, as reflected in the quote below, but during the last few years this seems to be a less serious problem. This sentiment is echoed by Transparency International[15] which reports that the Czech Republic has improved their rating significantly since 2005, and is now ranked 4.8 (in a range from zero to ten, with zero indicating no corruption and ten a highly corrupt environment). This is also illustrated by Robert Raschman, stating that 'Business is usually tendered publicly, but sometimes the process isn't always regulated properly, there is room for corruption, so this negatively effects our growth. It has improved slightly now.'

CONCLUSION

The case of Dekonta demonstrates several features of the innovation process within a specific setting: the waste management sector in the Czech Republic. This chapter has provided an overview of the opportunities and constraints resulting from the transition process, for instance the role of the mass privatization programme in creating an infrastructure which enabled

SMEs to flourish. At the same time, the Czech Republic has suffered from some setbacks in the development of an entrepreneurial culture, as under central planning the Czech economy was subject to almost complete government control, making reforms particularly difficult at the outset of transition.

Despite these difficulties the knowledge-based economy in the Czech Republic is slowly becoming established, with business expenditure on R&D and employment in mid to high-tech manufacturing reaching respectable levels. Moreover, a new Innovation Policy has been implemented with the broad aims of improving R&D and innovation performance.

The role of the enabling environment and how these factors have evolved over time has also been explored. Relationships are highly important for Dekonta and so far it has successfully adopted the network-based model of innovation (Pyka and Küppers 2002). Dekonta has collaborated with domestic competitors in several environmental projects, and it is also using partnerships to assist with its international activities in order to bring Dekonta's innovative activities to foreign markets.

An ambitious internationalization strategy has also been initiated at Dekonta, and this has become more important throughout the life of the firm. Currently, Dekonta enjoys a competitive advantage in Eastern markets due to lower overall cost structures and language competencies. However, over time the focus on Asia may become a limitation to its growth strategy; in the long term they may also need to consider Western markets in order to help them upgrade their product and service portfolio. Another strategic prescription can be suggested with regards to Dekonta's domestic diversification programme. In order to deal with the issue of domestic decline in some of Dekonta's initial services it may be beneficial to focus on their new set of services and facilities.

The case study also reveals the importance of the political and legal environments in creating the initial demand for Dekonta's environmental technologies through the privatization process. As for the influence of EU accession upon the demand for Dekonta's services this has not had a significant impact upon the firm's growth process. Instead, Dekonta has focused on Asian markets, as opposed to seeking customers in Western Europe. However, government policy has also posed some problems for the growth process of Dekonta, primarily in the form of excessive regulation in the approval process of new technologies. Thus it appears that in the case of Dekonta the government has played a dual role in the growth process and is a source of both constraints and opportunities for Dekonta's development.

Lastly, an important feature of Dekonta's strong innovation performance is an internal resource: the efficient use of its human capital base and the formation of cohesive teams, which work well together and encourage the exchange of information. These factors have remained crucial throughout the life cycle of the firm.

Therefore, to summarize, Dekonta has successfully used several aspects of the transition environment, in particular the legacy of strong human capital and the impetus of government demand for its environmental services. Dekonta has also made good use of networks and relationships in both the domestic and international markets. The domestic market is now facing saturation, but the implementation of a successful internationalization process means that the future remains promising for Dekonta.

ACKNOWLEDGEMENTS

This chapter was carried out under the auspices of the Knowledge, entrepreneurship, innovation, networks and systems STREP project under the direction of Professor Franco Malerba, CESPRI, University of Bocconi, Milan. I am grateful to the staff at Dekonta for making me welcome. Thanks also to Kristina Kadlecikova at the Technology Centre in Prague and to Karel Muller and Anna Kaderabkova at VSEM, Prague for their insights on the knowledge-based economy in the Czech Republic. Participants at the KEINS project workshop provided me with useful comments.

NOTES

1. a.s. is the abbreviation for akciova spolecnost and translates as joint stock company.
2. See http://www.euractiv.com/en/agenda2004/lisbon-agenda/article-117510 for more details.
3. Bioremediation is the use of living organisms to clean up oil spills, or for the removal of other pollutants from soil and water.
4. In February 2006 semi-structured interviews were carried out with Dekonta's core employees and the top management team. The 20-page questionnaire for the top management team covered the following: financial sources, evolution of the firm, relationships, strategy and performance. As for the 3-page questionnaire designed for core employees, this covered human capital issues, strategic changes within the firm and perceptions of the knowledge-based economy. I carried out a total of 10 interviews at Dekonta, three with the top management team and seven with the core employees: technicians, project managers, hydrogeologists and environmental engineers.
5. In 1983 the private sector produced 3.3 per cent of net material product (Mládek 1993).
6. The large-scale privatization process was carried out through a voucher system and was applied to most state-owned assets in industry.
7. In 1995 total spending on waste reached $100 million USD (REC Market Report).
8. The 'Black Triangle' refers to the heavily industrialized area between Poland, the Czech Republic and former East Germany.
9. Staff numbers are expected to grow in the future. The Romanian and Turkish subsidiaries and joint ventures are currently in their early stages of development.

10. Ústi nad Labem is situated in the north of the country and has a large concentration of coal mines and chemical plants and is therefore an ideal location for a waste treatment centre.
11. These include Geolink Consulting, ELC Group Ltd and CEVA respectively.
12. Atmogeochemical processes refer to the identification of volatile organic compounds.
13. ELC is a firm specializing in geotechnical and environmental geotechnology that operates out of Istanbul, Turkey.
14. US troops used herbicides to destroy vegetation that was being used as cover by Vietnamese soldiers. These herbicides contained dioxin and approximately 10 per cent of land in Vietnam is contaminated with it.
15. See http://www.transparency.org/content/download/8101/51449/file/Tiar 2005.pdf.

REFERENCES

Aidis, R. (2005), 'Entrepreneurship in Transition Economies: A Review', Centre for the Study of Economic and Social Change in Europe, Working Paper No. 61, SSEES, University College London, UK.

Baum, J., T. Calabrese and B. Silverman (2000), 'Don't Go It Alone: Alliance Network Composition and Startups' Performance in Canadian Technology', *Strategic Management Journal*, **21**, 267–94.

Begley, T., W. Tan and H. Schoch (2005), 'Politico-Economic Factors Associated with Interest in Starting a Business: A Multi-Country Study', *Entrepreneurship Theory and Practice*, **29** (1), 35–55.

Bohatá, M. and J. Mládek (1999), 'The Development of the Czech SME Sector', *Journal of Business Venturing*, **14** (5), 461–73.

Brummack, J. and A. Polster (2006), Patent Application for 'Methods for Drying Biomass', WO/2006/024463, World Intellectual Property Organisation, Switzerland, http://www.wipo.int/portal/index.html.en, accessed autumn 2006.

Coviello, N. and H. Munro (1997), 'Network Relationships and the Internationalisation Process of Small Software Firms', *International Business Review*, **6** (4), 361–86.

Dyba, K. and J. Svejnar (1995), 'A Comparative View of Economic Developments in the Czech Republic', in Jan Svejnar (ed.), *The Czech Republic and Economic Transition in Eastern Europe*, San Diego, CA: Academic Press Inc., pp. 21–47.

EBRD (2005), *Transition Report 2005: Business in Transition*, London: EBRD.

Ernst and Young (2006), *Doing Business in the Czech Republic through the Eyes of Czech Entrepreneurs*, Prague, Czech Republic.

European Commission (2003), *European Trend Chart on Innovation: Annual Innovation Policy Report for the Czech Republic*, Enterprise Directorate General, 2003/4.

Euroactiv.com (2004), 'Lisbon Agenda', Policy Section, downloaded from http://www.euractiv.com/en/agenda2004/lisbon-agenda/article-117510.

Grabher, Gernot and David Stark (eds) (1997), *Restructuring Networks in Post Socialism: Legacies, Linkages and Localities*, Oxford: Oxford University Press.

Grant, R. (1996), 'Toward a Knowledge Based Theory of the Firm', *Strategic Management Journal*, **4**, 109–22.

Lynn, M. (1998), 'Patterns of Micro-Enterprise Diversification in Transitional Eurasian Economies', *International Small Business Journal*, **16** (2), 34–49.

McDermott, G. (1991), 'Renegotiating the Ties that Bind: The Limits of Privatisation in the Czech Republic', Discussion Paper FSI 94-101, Berlin: WZB.

Mládek, J. (1993), 'Czech Small Privatisation: The Heyday is Over', *Czechoslovak Privatisation Newsletter*, No. 12, 1–5.

Nonaka, I. (1994), 'A Dynamic Theory of Organisational Knowledge Creation', *Organisation Science*, **5**, 14–37.

OECD (1996), *Small Businesses in Transition Economies. The Development of Enterprises in the Czech Republic, Hungary, Poland and Slovak Republic*, Paris: OECD.

Pyka, A. and G. Küppers (2002), *Innovation Networks: Theory and Practice*, Cheltenham, UK and Northampton, MA, USA: Edward Elgar.

REC (Regional Environmental Centre) (1997), 'The Environmental Technology Market in Central and Eastern Europe: An Overview of the Czech Republic, Hungary, Poland, Slovakia and Slovenia', Hungary.

Svejnar, J. (1995), 'A comparative view of economic development in the Czech Republic', in Jan Svejnar (ed.), *The Czech Republic and Economic Transition in Eastern Europe*, San Diego, CA: Academic Press Inc, Chapter 1.

Transparency International (2005), *Annual Report*, London.

Uhlíř, D. (1998), 'Internationalisation and Institutions and Regional Change: Restructuring Post Communist Networks in the Region of Lanskoun, Czech Republic', *Regional Studies*, **38**, 673–88.

UNECE (2006), 'Statistics Data Online', http://www.unece.org/stats/data.htm, accessed autumn 2006.

UNECE (2005), 'SME Databank', http://www.unece.org/indust/sme/smepub03.pdf, accessed autumn 2006.

UNIDO (2001), *SMEs: A Comparative Analysis of SME Strategies, Policies and Progress in Central European Initiative Countries*, UNIDO, Vienna.

Van de Ven, A. (1994), 'The Development of an Infrastructure for Entrepreneurship', *Journal of Business Venturing*, **8** (3), 211–30.

World Bank (2006), 'Doing Business Indicators', http://www.doingbusiness.org, accessed autumn 2006.

3. 'Matter-of-fact' entrepreneurship: FILKAB Joint Stock Company, Bulgaria

Tatiana S. Manolova

INTRODUCTION

Economies in transition have lately seen a rapid rise in entrepreneurship. During the 1990s, about 5 per cent of the adult working population in these countries attempted to start a new business or to become self-employed, a figure very similar to the percentage of nascent entrepreneurs in the United States and Western Europe (Peng 2001). Private small and medium-sized enterprises account for as much as 80 per cent of the GDP of countries such as the Czech Republic, the Slovak Republic, Estonia or Hungary, almost as much as in the industrialized West (EBRD 2005). Entrepreneurship is seen as a major engine for job creation and social change in these economies. That new and small entrepreneurial firms realize their full innovation and growth potential is therefore an important managerial and public policy concern.

Most of what we know about entrepreneurship in transition economies centres around the costs and constraints to entry and growth. Prior research, in particular, has extensively explored the negative effect of the underdeveloped and uncertain institutional environment (Peng 2001; Puffer and McCarthy 2001). Relatively less is known about the individual-level, firm-level, and environmental factors which enhance entrepreneurial performance in the context of transition economies. The present study seeks to address this gap by offering an in-depth look at the evolution and key success factors for an entrepreneurial venture in the cable distribution sector of the Bulgarian economy. It focuses, in particular, on the role and interplay of the founding team, the strategy, and the unique institutional context. The choice of a low-technology company allows the findings from the in-depth case study to be related to a broader group of companies, which operate not only in the 'glamorous' pockets of high growth and innovation, but also in the 'economic core' (Kirchhoff 1994).

The chapter is structured as follows. It starts by presenting an overview of the Bulgarian economy and the role of small and medium-sized enterprises (SMEs), with an emphasis on growth-oriented new ventures. It next presents the case context, followed by the key findings from the in-depth case study. The study concludes by discussing the role of the individual-level, firm-level, and environmental factors for entrepreneurial success, and their research and managerial implications.

PRIVATE ENTREPRENEURSHIP IN BULGARIA

Overview

Bulgaria is a lower-middle income country in Eastern Europe. Its economy is in the mid-stage of market and institutional reforms. Large-scale institutional and economic reforms started after the fall of the Berlin Wall (1989), and the country embarked on a road of transition to democratization and market liberalization.

Socialist central planning virtually eliminated the private sector of the economy for more than 40 years (from the late 1940s to 1989). Private businesses became legal in 1988 and have grown rapidly since then. The World Bank estimates that the growth of private business formation in Bulgaria outstripped the rates in countries such as Hungary or Poland (World Bank 2000). For example, there were 202 000 companies registered in Bulgaria in 2002 (of which 99.7 per cent were small and medium-sized), compared to 56 000 companies registered in Hungary, a country with a comparable population size (ASME 2004). In 2002, small and medium-sized enterprises in Bulgaria accounted for 45.6 per cent of the total gross value added and for as much as 66.5 per cent of the total employment in the economy (ASME 2004). Although growing, the contribution of SMEs to the Bulgarian economy has not yet reached its full potential. In Lithuania, Latvia, Poland, the Czech Republic and Hungary, for example, SMEs exceeded 40 per cent of the gross value added as early as the mid-1990s (ASME 2004). Table 3.1 compares Bulgaria's key economic indicators to other Central and Eastern European countries, while Table 3.2 summarizes the role of the SMEs in the Bulgarian economy.

One reason for the lower contribution of SMEs to the Bulgarian economy relative to other New Europe entrepreneurial ventures may be the severity of economic disruption caused by the large-scale structural reforms. By 2001, Bulgaria had reached only 74 per cent of its pre-transition (1989) level of economic activity. In comparison, the five most developed Central European transition economies had increased their combined output to 115 per cent of

Table 3.1   Bulgaria: key economic indicators relative to other New Europe economies

	Bulgaria	Czech R.	Estonia	Hungary	Latvia	Lithuania	Poland	Romania	Slovak R.	Slovenia
Population (millions)	7.8	10.2	1.4	10.1	2.3	3.4	38.2	21.7	5.4	2
Area ('000 sq.km)	111	78.9	45	93	64.5	67	313.9	238	49	20.5
GDP (billion US$ 2004)	24.1	107	11.2	100.3	13.5	22.3	241.8	73.2	41.1	32.2
GDP per cap in 2004 at current international US$ (PPP)	8026	19311	13740	16596	11962	12994	12876	8413	14549	20853
Private sector share in GDP in 2005 (%)	70	80	80	80	70	75	75	70	80	65
Inflation 2005 estimation (%)	4.2	2	3.9	3.8	6.4	2.8	2.2	9.2	2.4	2.5
Unemployment rate (UNECE 2003) (%)	13.6	7.8	10.1	5.8	10.5	12.7	19.2	6.6	17.1	6.5
FDI inflows 2004 (as a % of GDP)	5.1	3.7	7	3.6	4	2.3	2	3.1	1	3.3
Est. level of real GDP in 2004[a]	89	114	112	120	90	89	142	100	121	126

Note: a.   The estimated level of real GDP in 2004 is compared to the base year 1989 = 100.

Sources: EBRD (2005); UNECE (http:www.unece.org).

Table 3.2   Small and medium-sized enterprises in the Bulgarian economy, 2002 (%)

Categories	Number of enterprises	Total sales	Total value added	Total employment
Micro (1–9)	90.8	23.7	11.8	25.9
Small (10–49)	7.3	21.3	14.8	18.9
Medium (50–249)	1.6	21.0	19.0	21.7
Large (250 +)	0.3	34.0	54.4	33.5
Sectoral distribution[a]				
Extraction	0.1			
Manufacturing	12.0			
Utilities	0.04			
Construction	4.1			
Trade and repairs	55.4			
Hotels and restaurants	10.2			
Transport and communications	7.7			
Real estate and business services	10.4			

Note: a. Employment category 1–99 only.

Source: ASME (2004).

the 1989 levels (World Bank 2005). The abrupt substitution of the planned state economy with a market-based exchange system over a relatively short period of time led to excessive and persistent unemployment, which in turn decreased the opportunity costs of self-employment and resulted in large-scale predominantly necessity-based entrepreneurship (Acs et al. 2004). As could be expected, more than half (55.4 per cent) of the new ventures in Bulgaria are being started in retail and repairs, a sector with low barriers to entry and limited potential for differentiation, innovation, growth and value creation (Scase 1997; Kirchhoff 1994).

Another reason may be traced to the perceived unfavourable impact of the institutional environment. Interestingly, the objective regulatory barriers to entrepreneurial entry and the costs of doing business in Bulgaria are not significantly different from other New Europe economies. According to the World Bank's most recent 'Doing Business' indicators (World Bank 2006b), the costs of doing business in Bulgaria are about the same or better than the average for the region. Thus, it takes 7.9 per cent of per capita income to start a business, compared to the region's average of 14.1 per cent, and 9 per cent of the estate to close a business, compared to the region's average of 14.3 per cent. Notably, Bulgaria boasts the best public credit registry coverage at 20.7 per cent of all adults, considerably higher than the region's average of 1.7 per cent. Yet, Bulgarian managers appear more sceptical about the level of institutional support for business development relative to their Central European and Baltic counterparts. According to the World Bank's most recent World Development Indicators, a considerably higher percentage of Bulgarian managers view crime, coupled with corruption and an ineffective court system, as major business constraints (World Bank 2006a). Bulgarian managers are particularly concerned about the inability of courts to uphold property rights. Thus, 56.7 per cent of the Bulgarian managers who participated in the World Bank survey responded that they lacked confidence in courts to uphold property rights (the highest percentage in the region), compared to 29.6 per cent of the Estonian managers surveyed (the lowest percentage in the region).

Not surprisingly, Bulgarian private entrepreneurs depend to a large extent on informal norms for security (Peng 2004; Khanna and Palepu 1997) and maintain a low profile and a short-term outlook. Kirov and Stoeva (2005), in an in-depth study of small businesses' growth motivations, found persistent socio-cultural barriers to growth. These barriers were rooted in both personal preferences and environmental influences, such as the personal trajectories of the entrepreneurs' behaviour, the limited access to business development services, and employment relations based on the trust in friends or family circles. Table 3.3 presents comparative aspects of the country's institutional profile for entrepreneurship.

Growth-oriented Entrepreneurial Ventures in Bulgaria

Growth-oriented entrepreneurial ventures in Bulgaria differ from the typical small enterprise in several critical aspects. To start with, they differ in the level of human capital embedded in their founders. The Bulgarian high-growth entrepreneur is likely to have a college education (typically in engineering or the sciences), as well as industry and managerial experience, usually in a large state-owned enterprise. In contrast, the typical small-business owner has secondary or vocational secondary education, with some (not necessarily managerial) experience in a state-owned enterprise or the state administration (Todorov 2001; Ministry of Economy and Energy 2005). Equally important, more than half of the high-growth entrepreneurial ventures in Bulgaria are started in manufacturing (Todorov 2001) rather than retail. Manufacturing offers a much higher potential for innovation, differentiation, growth and value added. Case studies of high performing Bulgarian entrepreneurial ventures showcase companies in several industrial clusters, such as wineries, timber or tourism, which benefit from the country's factor conditions and location advantages (ASME 2002).

Table 3.3 *Bulgaria: institutional environment for entrepreneurship, 2005*

	Bulgaria	Czech R.	Estonia	Hungary	Latvia	Lithuania	Poland	Romania	Slovak R.	Slovenia	Region	OECD
Doing business indicators[a]												
Starting a business (% per cap income)	7.9	8.9	5.1	20.9	3.5	2.8	21.4	4.4	4.8	9.4	14.1	5.3
Dealing with licences (% per cap income)	270.5	14.5	34.3	260	36.3	18.2	85.6	332.6	17.1	122.2	564.9	72
Hiring workers (% salary)	30.1	35	33.5	35.2	24.1	31.2	21.4	33	35.2	16.6	26.7	21.4
Firing costs (weeks of wages)	8.7	21.7	34.7	34.5	17.3	30.3	13	3	13	39.6	26.2	31.3
Registering property (% property value)	2.3	3	0.7	11	2	0.7	2	1.9	0.1	2	2.7	4.3
Public credit registry coverage (% adults)	20.7	3.5	0	0	1.9	4.2	0	2.6	1	2.9	1.7	8.4
Total tax rate (% profit)	40.7	49	50.2	59.3	42.6	48.4	38.4	48.9	48.9	39.4	56	47.8
Enforcing a contract (% debt)	14	14.1	11.5	9.6	11.8	8.6	10	10.7	15.7	15.2	15	11.2
Closing a business (% estate)	9	14.5	9	14.5	13	7	22	9	18	8	14.3	7.1
Managerial perceptions[b]												
Corruption (% of managers ranking this as a major business constraint)	19	20.5	4.3	9.4	9.6	14	18.2	30.1	10.6	3.7		

Table 3.3 (continued)

	Bulgaria	Czech R.	Estonia	Hungary	Latvia	Lithuania	Poland	Romania	Slovak R.	Slovenia	Region OECD
Courts (% of managers lacking confidence in courts to uphold property rights)	56.7	53.1	29.6	49.5	51.3	49.7	47.4	44.3	44.4	34.4	
Courts (% of managers ranking this as a major business constraint)	17.2	25.2	2	7.4	5.8	15.3	21	19.7	13.1	8.1	
Crime (% of managers ranking this as a major business constraint)	11.5	15.8	1.9	5.6	3.1	9.5	15	15.3	5.1	0.9	

Source: a. From http://www.doingbusiness.org/ExploreEconomies/; b. World Bank (2006a).

More recently, a renewed public policy emphasis is being placed on the performance of the high-technology sector. It is acknowledged that the lack of funding coupled with the absence of a clearly articulated government policy has had a detrimental effect on technology development and innovation. As of 2003, Bulgaria trailed most New Europe economies in the level of both public and public R&D expenditures (European Commission 2005). A 1999 representative study found that only 0.6 per cent of the small and medium-sized enterprises in the country spent over 5 per cent on R&D (ASME 2000). Not surprisingly, innovation output was severely affected. Thus, only 3.7 high-tech patent applications (per million population) submitted to the European Patent Office in 2002 originated from Bulgaria, compared to 32.8 (per million population) from Slovenia, a country with a quarter of the population of Bulgaria. Based on the 2005 Summary Innovation Index, compiled by the European Commission, Bulgaria ranked twenty-sixth out of 33 surveyed countries (European Commission 2005). Table 3.4 presents comparative aspects of the country's innovation scoreboard.

As of 2002, microelectronics has been recognized as a high-technology cluster with excellent growth and export potential. Its development is based on the tradition, experience and existing production facilities in the country. Other contributing factors include the availability of highly-educated and well-qualified hardware and software engineers.

Against the background of small and medium-sized enterprise development in Bulgaria, and the growth-oriented entrepreneurial sector in particular, the rest of the chapter will offer an in-depth look at a successful growth-oriented Bulgarian entrepreneurial venture. The choice of a company which operates in a relatively low-technology industrial sector such as cable distribution allows us to generalize the findings from the in-depth case study to a broader group of companies across industrial sectors. The study highlights the role of a cohesive team spirit, realistic strategy making and persistent strategy execution for successful entrepreneurial performance and growth in transition economies.

FILKAB JSCO: THE CASE OF 'MATTER-OF-FACT' ENTREPRENEURSHIP

FILKAB Joint Stock Company (JSCo) is located in Plovdiv, the second largest Bulgarian city. It distributes cables, wires and electrical equipment, offering over 22 000 product items, as well as engineering services, including in-house assembly of electric panels, transformer substations, distribution switchboards and lighting systems. The company is ISO 9001 certified[1] and is a distributor for over 20 global manufacturers, such as Tyco

Table 3.4 Bulgaria: innovation scoreboard

	Bulgaria	Czech R.	Estonia	Hungary	Latvia	Lithuania	Poland	Romania	Slovak R.	Slovenia	EU15	US
Public R&D expenditures (% of GDP)[a]	0.39	0.50	0.53	0.62	0.25	0.54	0.43	0.17	0.24	0.63	0.69	0.76
Business R&D expenditures (% of GDP)[b]	0.10	0.77	0.28	0.36	0.14	0.14	0.16	0.23	0.23	0.90	1.3	2.04
European Patent Office high-tech patent applications (per million population)[c]	3.7	10.9	8.9	18.3	6.0	2.6	2.7	0.9	4.3	32.8	31.6	57.0

Notes: a. 2003 except Slovak Republic, 2004; b. 2003 except Slovak Republic, 2004; c. 2002 except EU15 and US, 2003.

Source: European Commission (2005).

Electronics (USA), Siemens and Nexans (Germany), and Schneider Electric (France). As of July 2006, FILKAB boasted annualized sales of over €27 million, close to 200 employees, and a customer base of over 3000 clients, commanding a 25 per cent share of the domestic market.

Interviews with the six company owners provided the major source of data for the case study. The interviews lasted between one and one-and-a-half hours and were semi-structured, allowing for a lot of open-ended questions. Method triangulation was used to enhance the reliability of the findings. In particular, primary data collected through the interviews were complemented by site observations and study of company documents, government publications, and the national business press (Yin 1993).

The interview protocol consisted of five sets of questions: (1) the history of the company's founding, initial vision and strategies; (2) major milestones and crises and how these marked the development of the firm; (3) vision and strategy for the future, major opportunities and threats; (4) criteria for and satisfaction with venture performance, key factors contributing to the success of the venture; and (5) the role of the institutional environment in the evolution of the venture. To aid in data consistency, the interview data were coded based on typical content analysis procedures (Miles and Huberman 1984) into each of the following coding categories: (1) characteristics of the founder(s); (2) role of vision and strategy; and (3) environmental enabling factors.

The Company: History and Major Development Milestones

The company beginnings can be traced to the early 1990s, right after the fall of the Berlin Wall, and to three neighbours, who knew each other well. One of the three friends invited his boss to join their entrepreneurial initiative, and the boss agreed. Thus, FILCOM-4 was registered in 1990 as a general partnership of four partners (two economists and two engineers). The company had BGL 1700 in start-up capital, drawn from personal and family savings.

From the outset, the founders agreed on several principles that would guide their activities. First, they decided to enter trade in cables, wires and electrical supplies. The rationale for the choice of the line of business was that the maintenance of the electricity supply infrastructure is as important as the supply of basic commodities. In addition, cables, wires and electrical supplies are durable goods that can be kept in stock over long periods of time. The three partners could also leverage existing contacts with suppliers and end users of the products. Next, they decided that three of them would leave their current employment to work full-time for the private company, whereas the fourth, who was at the time employed at a local bank, would continue with his employment in order to facilitate obtaining bank financing, if necessary. Finally, they set up the goal of reaching BGL 40 000 in revenues for the first year.

There are three cable and wire producing plants in Bulgaria, in Smolyan, Sevlievo, and Bourgas. The first commercial transaction was carried out with the Sevlievo plant, and after a couple of successful transactions paid in cash upon receipt, the partners negotiated getting the goods on a thirty-day credit. Thus, they introduced consignment trade in cables and electrical supplies. One of the founders recollects: 'The director of Sevlievo was the first one to realize that distribution was starting to suffer because of the collapse of the state owned wholesale companies, and he was willing to try private distributors on consignment. We took advantage of this moment.'

A big boost in revenues came with the start of market liberalization in 1991. The big state-owned cable distributors had no flexibility to react to market supply and demand, failing to realize that the market prices were 5–6 times higher than the 'planned' prices they were selling at. In 1991, encouraged by the successful start, the founders transformed the partnership into a limited liability company (LLC), as per the new Commercial Law.

For the next eight years, the company grew at a steady pace, adding new items to the product mix, and attracting both state-owned and newly formed private companies as customers and suppliers. It acquired its own commercial fleet of vehicles, relocated several times to new and larger warehousing facilities, and added between 10–15 new employees each year. Growth was conservatively financed by internally generated funds. The four founders managed all aspects of the company operations themselves. The only unrelated diversification initiative was undertaken in 1993, when the company acquired the assets of a timber processing mill from a liquidated agricultural cooperative in the village of Slaveino, in the Rhodope mountains. As one of the founders explains: 'The Slaveino deal was purely opportunistic, it occurred because of a provision in the tax code. Fixed assets investments were tax deductible and we took advantage of a state farm being liquidated. Any rational businessman would prefer to invest the money instead of paying a tax on it. The financial motivation prevailed over the strategic motivation in this instance.'

Toward the end of the 1990s, the founders started looking to buy their own warehouse facilities. One of the partners tells the story:

> The director of our bank offered us to buy a cession, assuming the outstanding debt of a delinquent borrower. We could present it to the court and have a priority claim on the mortgaged property. At the beginning we had some misgivings because that debt instrument was not very popular in Bulgaria at the time. But we decided to take the risk, bought the outstanding debt, and presented the cession to the court. The court ruled in our favour, and we came into possession

of the warehouse. The procedure was not very clear-cut, and there were other candidates keen to get the warehouse once the court proceeded with the liquidation. Fortunately we had the cession, which gave us a priority claim on the collateral, and also gave us the right to buy the warehouse at 80 per cent of the appraised value. But it was far from automatic. It took us 5–6 months before we could move in.

By 1999, the founders began to realize that the company, which had reached BGL 28 million (€14 million) in sales, was outgrowing its managerial and organizational structure. They then reorganized their activities into three separate companies: FILKAB JSCo, which assumed the distribution of cables and wires; FILTECH JSCo, which assumed the distribution for Tyco Electronic's German subsidiary Raychem GmbH; and FILCOM-4, which continued managing the rest of the company's activities, and also held the title to all real estate. The founders held the majority stock in all of the companies, however in both FILKAB and FILTECH stock was offered to key partners and executive officers. This amalgamation of governance structures did not prove effective. As one of the partners recollects:

The division was a mistake, not the division as an idea but the way we technically implemented it. We should not have created FILKAB as a separate company from FILCOM, but rather FILCOM should have created FILKAB. Frictions between different activities started to appear. Having worked in this manner for two to three years, we definitely saw the need to restructure and put the company back together. Everyone makes mistakes, the important thing is to learn from one's mistakes.

By 2002, FILKAB JSCo had begun the process of assuming all of the spawned companies' assets and stock. The owners expected the process to continue through 2006.

Also in 1999, the newly formed FILKAB JSCo was faced with a major challenge. Elcabel Bourgas, the biggest cable manufacturer in Bulgaria, and the only Bulgarian producer of high voltage power cables, was privatized, and unilaterally cancelled its distribution contract with the company. FILKAB had to find an alternative supplier, fast, if it wanted to continue to be a player in the lucrative power cable business. In the words of one of the owners:

This was a very difficult year for FILKAB, because we had to find foreign cable manufacturers and become their distributors on the Bulgarian market. The next challenges were the specifications. All technical specifications our clients worked with were based on the Bulgarian standard. So it was very painful at the beginning to convince our clients that the foreign analogues corresponded to the Bulgarian standard. Now things are different and we can say we developed the import sector in this market, now we sell probably 70 per cent Bulgarian and 30 per cent imported cables. To achieve this, in 2000 we decided to compile a comparative catalogue, which is unique for the country. It's now a desktop reference for project managers, engineers, students, etc., and is in its sixth edition. It turned out that this is the best advertisement for our company. People look for us after they get hold of the catalogue. We can say we educated our Bulgarian partners through this catalogue.

As of mid-2006, FILKAB JSCo looks to the future with optimism and determination. Ivan Kukov, the executive director, outlines the strategy for growth: 'Diversification is a good word, but you cannot be an expert in too many different areas of business. Even though you can spread risk, you still need good expertise in every line of business in order to be able to manage them all well. It's a question of resources, as well as the link with the existing businesses. New opportunities are always considered, but not at any cost, they need to fit within the specialization of the company.'

Although all company owners were unanimous that FILKAB (together with its predecessor) has been a very successful company, they provided complementary perspectives on what success meant to them. These perspectives included 'realization of what has been planned and envisioned', 'high growth rate', a 'good image', 'the ascending development curve without any jolts and crises'. Founders also emphasized 'the preservation of the founding team' as a measure of success. Table 3.5 provides a detailed company timeline, whereas Table 3.6 offers a summary of the company's financial performance over the past four years.

KEY FINDINGS

The case findings are organized so as to highlight the main constructs of interest to the study, namely (1) characteristics of the founder(s); (2) role of vision and strategy; and (3) environmental enabling factors.

Characteristics of the Founding Team

The four founders boasted high levels of human capital in terms of both education and experience. At the time the new venture was established, between them they had eight degrees (one master's) and 48 years of work experience, including 25 years of industry-specific experience and close to 20 years of managerial experience. This experience was invaluable in setting up the parameters of the new venture. One of the founders explains: 'Although it operated under the socialist rules, the way of the product from the manufacturer to the ultimate customer was clear to us. Few people

Table 3.5   FILKAB JSCo's timeline

1990	FILCOM-4 general partnership established in Plovdiv, Bulgaria. Consignment contract signed with EMKA Sevlievo.
1991	Partnership transformed into an LLC Leases commercial space from the regional state-owned distributor (OPSO) of cables and electrical supplies. Buys a used truck and a van, and a PC. Hires its first employee (a truck driver). Starts own delivery. Fourth partner leaves his jobs and assumes responsibility for accounting and finance. Consignment contract signed with Gammacable Smolyan.
1992	Leases office and retail space. Opens a retail store and hires two more employees. Broadens the product mix. Consignment contract signed with Elcabel Bourgas.
1993	Acquires the assets of a liquidated agricultural cooperative in the village of Slaveino. Starts manufacturing of timber, flooring, windows, and doors.
1994	OPSO refuses to renew the lease. FILCOM-4 moves to new warehouses leased from the Packaging Machines plants.
1997	Acquires its own warehouses by assuming the debt of ISKRA, a state-owned company which defaults on its credit payments.
1998	Opens branch in Veliko Turnovo. Wins the 'Taxpayer of the Year' award.
1999	The owners split business in three companies. FILKAB JSCo offers stock to two newly hired executives, bringing the total number of owners to six.
2001	Gets ISO 9001 certification. Wins its second 'Taxpayer of the Year' award.
2002	Wins its third 'Taxpayer of the Year' award.
2004	Begins production of electric panels, adds a design group. Opens a branch in Sliven.
2005	Opens an office in Sofia.
2006	Opens branches in Bourgas and Rousse.

knew that, and we knew that professionally. We knew what product was produced at what cost, the structure of the mark-ups, the need for warehousing and logistics, we knew all that.'

Perhaps more importantly, the industry experience brought with it valuable contacts, leading to high levels of social capital. As one of the founders points out, 'If you know people, you can develop a business; if you don't

Table 3.6   FILKAB JSCo: performance highlights (thousand BGL^a^ *)*

Indicator	2002	2003	2004	2005
Net sales	23 679	31 528	44 150	54 442
Net income	1 236	1 505	4 276	5 019
Equity	3 428	4 804	8 757	13 350
Assets	7 975	11 369	16 453	25 420

Note: a. Since 1999, the Bulgarian lev has been pegged to the euro (1 BGL = €0.5113).

Source: Company Annual Reports.

know people, you may know a lot about the industry, but you won't have a business.'

In addition, the human and social capital of the start-up team was well balanced. In terms of expertise, the founding team's education and experience covered both the technical and the financial side of the business. In terms of social capital, it afforded the founders both depth and breadth, complementing personal contacts in the cable sector with a network of contacts in banking, research and development, and related industries. This allowed the founders to professionally manage their start-up on their own. It was only when the business reached a critical size threshold that the need for strengthening the professional management was felt. The newly joining owners brought an even higher level of specialized education, industry and managerial experience. Table 3.7 presents the six owners' profiles.

Interestingly, when founders reflected on the role of the human factor, they emphasized the team characteristics, rather than the personal endowments of the individual team members. In the words of one of the founders:

> What helped us survive and prosper is that in the toughest moments we've always been in a fist. And no one got greedy. I think the other companies failed because there were conflicts among partners, they started lying to each other and stealing from each other and so on. We devoted all efforts to the development of the company, and we have no regrets about that . . . It's difficult to say if we would have been successful in any business. Maybe we would not have been as successful if we started in apparel, for example. But I believe the team is good and we would have made it in any business.

Role of Vision and Strategy

The approach to strategy formulation was steady and step-by-step. As one of the founders describes it: 'The initial goal was not to grow big, but to sustain ourselves. Nothing else. When we had enough to cover our living

Table 3.7 Owners' profiles

Name, gender, age when founded/joined company	Managerial position	Education	Experience	Note
Ivan Kukov, male, 35	Executive Director Member, BOD	BS Economics (Organization and Management of Industrial Production)	*Balkankar Assenovgrad* (1 yr); *Electrical Devices Assenovgrad* (5 yrs) *Electrical Devices Plovdiv* (5 yrs): Expert, HR; Director HR; Director, Planning; Deputy CEO, Business and Sales	Founder
Rumen Cankov, male, 37	Chairman, BOD	BS Engineering (Machine Engineering) BS Economics (Organization and Management of Machine Engineering) MS (Patents and Patent Law)	*High Power Transformers Plant Sofia* (1 yr): Production Manager *Contact Elements Plant Smolyan* (6 yrs): Designer; Manufacturing, Production, Planning Manager *Electrical Devices Plovdiv* (4 yrs): Engineering, Marketing Manager	Founder
Margarit Georgiev, male, 38	Member, BOD	BS Economics (Accounting) BS Economics (International Economic Relations)	'*George Dimitrov' Science & Production Complex Plovdiv* (13 yrs): Accountant, Economist, Head of Planning *Mineralbank Plovdiv* (5 yrs) : Chief Expert	Founder

Table 3.7 (continued)

Name, gender, age when founded/joined company	Managerial position	Education	Experience	Note
Latchezar Manolov, male, 33	Member, BOD	BS Engineering (Food Processing Equipment) BS Economics (Organization and Management of Machine Engineering)	*Cannery Plovdiv* (4 yrs): Chief Mechanic *Biotechnica Corp. Plovdiv* (2 yrs): Expert *Process Automation Research Center Plovdiv* (2 yrs): Head of Project Contract Department	Founder
Vasil Madanski, male, 47	Executive Director Director, Cables Member, BOD	BS Engineering (Plastics Manufacturing)	*Institute for Cables and Conductors, Smolyan branch* (7 yrs): rose to Deputy Head; *Gammacable Smolyan* (13 yrs): Deputy Managing Director, Manufacturing	Joined in 1999
Nikola Avramov, male, 50	Director, Planning Member, BOD	BS Engineering (Non-Ferrous MetalsTechnology)	*Non-Ferrous Metallurgy Plant Pirdop* (13 yrs) *Gammacable Smolyan* (22 yrs): Chief Technologist	Joined in 1999

46

expenses, when we bought our personal cars, which, for the first time in our lives, were different from the Soviet Ladas, we started accumulating money to buy our own warehouses. Our goals got bigger.'

Steady and deliberate in their approach as they were, the founders were not afraid to take risks and make strategic innovations. These included many 'market-firsts', such as the introduction of cable distribution on consignment or the introduction of imported cables into the domestic market. Interestingly, when asked if differentiation is possible for a standard-based, commodity product, such as cables, one of the executive directors offered the following rationale:

> Even though cables are a standard good, there are differences in the quality of materials. High quality inputs affect exploitation specifications and thus serve as points of differentiation. All colleagues define the Bulgarian market as price-driven. Nonetheless, we've never made a compromise on quality. We've always worked with reputable manufacturers. This determines the level of trust clients have towards our products and towards the company as a whole. This is probably one of our biggest competitive advantages.

As the company grew and evolved from an entrepreneurial new venture to a professionally managed company, it also introduced a formal planning cycle. One of the executive directors provides more detail: 'We have a long-term investment programme and also annual plans. We started the annual planning cycle a year before the ISO certification was initiated. We rarely update the annual business plans, because we have the experience needed to accurately forecast and plan within such a short horizon. Sometimes, however, we are overly conservative in our sales projections.'

One of the defining characteristics of the company is the consistency in strategy implementation. This is manifested in the utilization of a state-of-the-art information technology and the development of departmental objectives to constantly track sales and clients; a flexible organizational structure to respond to changing market conditions; and a formal system for training, evaluation, and development of human resources. Notably, fewer than ten employees have left the company over its sixteen-year long existence. The company prides itself on paying top wages, on offering comprehensive health and retirement benefits, on its strict compliance with labour and safety regulations, and on its democratic structure. As one of the owners explains: 'We have no secretaries, no receptionist. This was partly the response to space constraints. Both Executive Directors share offices with other employees. The only two people not sharing an office are the head of security and the head of the engineering department, partly because the engineering department is housed in a new wing of the building. To the outsider, this gives an impression of complete transparency.'

Role of the Institutional Environment

Interestingly, none of the interviewees considered the institutional environment as a major roadblock for the development of the company. In a very matter-of-fact manner, the company owners discussed institutions as 'good for now', 'a given that needs to be accounted for' and 'not an impediment to the development of the company'. One of the founders elaborated:

> Neither the constitution, nor the laws, nor the regulations were intentionally directed against the private sector development. True, we did not like a lot of things within the regulations, but I think that when we sum up the legacy of these 15 years, I don't think there has been a big intentional obstacle. The bad thing is that all of this could have been lived through much faster, maybe over 4 or 5 years. We all wanted changes to take effect fast and maybe be better implemented, but it turned out that they took much longer and were a lot more painful.

Indeed, FILKAB prides itself on its transparent reporting and compliance with state laws and local regulations. The company has won the Taxpayer of the Year award three times. This award is given annually by the Ministry of Finance for exemplary compliance with financial reporting standards. One of the founders voices the philosophy of the founding team: 'A lot of those who started with us did not make it, others became very successful, yet others ended with a bullet in their heads. We managed to remain in the respected, law-abiding business. We wanted to be a respectable, legal business from the start. Our idea from the beginning was that all business will be legal one day, and then we won't have to change anything.'

In terms of the enabling influence of the transition period, several themes emerged. Almost all of the interviewees emphasized the socialist investment in education, which afforded a 'much broader basis of knowledge which allows us to be more open to opportunities and be more flexible' and the 'discipline and compliance with rules'. Other than that, as one of the founders succinctly stated, 'Whoever worked hard under socialism, is working well today; whoever did not work hard under socialism, is not working today either.'

A unique advantage to starting fresh, according to the interviewees, may be the optimism and enthusiasm of 'creating something new'. As one of the executive directors remarked: 'In a fifty-year old company, you don't know how the firm was established and developed. In our company, everyone is excited to be creating something new. In an established firm things are already settled down and employees turn into bureaucrats.' This was echoed by one of the founders who stated that 'We've always been in a crisis mode, so we're not impressed. We're forever hopeful that tomorrow will be better than today. No matter how much we complain, we have a little of this pure optimism remaining. I think this will give us somewhat of an advantage.'

DISCUSSION

The goal of the in-depth case study was to highlight the specific aspects of the interplay between the individual entrepreneur, the new venture, and the institutional setting that created the enabling context for innovative entrepreneurial behaviour to develop and grow. The insights from the case study with respect to these three issues will be discussed next.

The Role of the Founders and the Founding Team

This study supports a long lineage of literature in entrepreneurship – and entrepreneurship in transition economies in particular – which has highlighted the critical importance of the founders' human and social capital for the survival, success, and growth of the new venture (Cooper et al. 1994; Bartlett and Rangelova 1997; Nahapiet and Ghoshal 1998; Peng 2001; Manev et al. 2005). Human capital is particularly important for small business in an environment characterized by rapid change (Honig 1998). Entrepreneurs with stronger preparation or those who can tap into the experience of others are more likely to be able to deal with uncertainty and with the numerous problems that arise as their ventures grow and develop (Cooper et al. 1994). Further, social capital is vital for the performance of new and small companies in the context of transition economies (Peng and Heath 1996; Xin and Pearce 1996) characterized by resource-scarcity and an unstable and weakly-structured environment (Peng 2001; Puffer and McCarthy 2001; Smallbone and Welter 2001).

Extending this line of research, the present study provides rich case evidence on the important role of the interactions between the team members as a critical success factor for the survival, growth, and success of the new venture. Notably, the preservation of the founding team was seen as one of the indicators of successful new venture performance. While the role of entrepreneurial founding teams has been extensively explored in the context of entrepreneurship in the developed market economies (Aldrich et al. 2004), it has not been sufficiently studied in the context of transition economies. Apparently, more research on this important aspect of the founding process is well warranted.

The Role of Strategy Formulation and Implementation

This study brought to the fore the critical role of strategy formulation and implementation for successful entrepreneurial performance and growth. It highlighted, in particular, the importance of realistic, 'matter-of-fact' establishment of strategic objectives and the even greater importance of persistent strategy execution. Notably, the findings from the study revealed that a legally-minded approach to compliance with formal and informal norms and a combination of compliance and balancing (Oliver 1991) is conducive to the success of an entrepreneurial venture in a transition economy.

These findings support Peng's (2003) argument that during the late stages of transitions start-ups are more likely to compete on competitive resources and capabilities. Similarly, recent research by Danis and Lyles (2004) suggests managerial networking behaviour appears to be a stronger predictor of firm performance early in transition but this influence wanes over time as competitive methods based on traditional conceptualizations of firm strategy become increasingly important.

In other words, as market-oriented reforms lead to a greater convergence between transition and developed market economies, the key success factors for entrepreneurial success and performance (Chandler and Hanks 1994) also tend to converge. An interesting question for future research will be to ascertain if subtle but distinct differences in strategic approaches and strategic choices between entrepreneurs from developed and transition economies will tend to persist over time.

The Transition Context as a Source of Competitive Advantage

Finally, the findings from the study suggest that the unique institutional context during the transition period may enable entrepreneurial ventures to develop distinct sources of competitive advantage. In particular, the high levels of development of human capital, coupled with the socialist legacy of considering the human resources of the company as its most valuable asset may allow a company to reap the benefits of the long-term investments in human capital, such as employee expertise, loyalty and commitment.

In addition, the unique opportunity to build and 'create something new' fosters an entrepreneurial spirit, which permeates the organization and leaves a lasting imprint on its culture. An intangible and socially complex resource such as organizational culture is both valuable and extremely hard to imitate and may serve as a source for sustainable competitive advantage. Future research should explore – in a large-scale empirical study or a matched-pair series of comparative case studies – the enabling role of the institutional context in creating competitive advantages for entrepreneurial ventures in transition economies.

CONCLUSIONS

The insights gleaned through the case study generally support previous research on the role of human and social capital, but suggest more research is warranted on the role of the start-up team for successful entrepreneurial performance in the context of a transition economy. Further, a greater emphasis on the role of strategy formulation and execution leads to higher levels of entrepreneurial performance. Finally, this study suggests that the socialist legacy of investment in human capital, coupled with the enthusiasm for creating something new may offer the entrepreneurs in transition economies a unique source of competitive advantage.

In conclusion, this study highlighted the fact that passionate entrepreneurial commitment, a cohesive team spirit, the ability to work with people, and the ability to learn from mistakes promote successful entrepreneurial performance and growth in transition economies. Perhaps more importantly, this study showed that hard work, realistic strategic objectives and a persistent and 'matter-of-fact' approach to strategy execution provide the basis for distinct and durable competitive advantage. While universal for new and small ventures across institutional contexts and industry structures, these simple lessons are particularly important for entrepreneurial ventures in New Europe as they enter the competitive vistas of the European market.

NOTE

1. The ISO 9000 family of standards is primarily concerned with 'quality management'. This means what the organization does to fulfil the customer's quality requirements and applicable regulatory requirements, while aiming to enhance customer satisfaction, and achieve continual improvement of its performance in pursuit of these objectives (www.iso.org).

REFERENCES

Acs, Z.J., P. Arenius, M. Hay and M. Minniti (2004), *Global Entrepreneurship Monitor: 2004 Executive Report*, Babson Park, MA: Babson College and London, UK: London Business School.

Agency for Small and Medium-Sized Enterprises (ASME) (2004), *Report on the Small and Medium-Sized Enterprises, 2002–2003*, Sofia, Bulgaria: ASME.

Agency for Small and Medium-Sized Enterprises (ASME) (2002), *Report on the Small and Medium-Sized Enterprises, 2000–2002*, Sofia, Bulgaria: ASME.

Agency for Small and Medium-Sized Enterprises (ASME) (2000), *Report on the Small and Medium-Sized Enterprises, 1996–1999*, Sofia, Bulgaria: ASME.

Aldrich, H.E., N.M. Carter and M. Ruef (2004), 'Teams', in W.B. Gartner, K.S. Shaver, N.M. Carter and P.D. Reynolds (eds), *Handbook of Entrepreneurial Dynamics: The Process of Business Creation*, Thousand Oaks, CA: Sage, pp. 299–310.

Bartlett, W. and R. Rangelova (1997), 'Small Firms and Economic Transformation in Bulgaria', *Small Business Economics*, **9** (4), 319–33.

Chandler, G. and S.H. Hanks (1994), 'Market Attractiveness, Resource-Based Capabilities, Venture Strategies, and Venture Performance', *Journal of Business Venturing*, **9** (4), 331–49.

Cooper, A.C., F.J. Gimeno-Gascon and C.Y. Woo (1994), 'Initial Human and Financial Capital as Predictors of New Venture Performance', *Journal of Business Venturing*, **9** (5), 371–95.

Danis, W.M. and M.A. Lyles (2004), 'A Longitudinal Study of Entrepreneurs in a Transition Economy: When Does Competitive Strategy Matter Most?', Paper presented at the JIBS/AIB Paper Development Workshop at the Academy of International Business Annual Meeting, Stockholm, Sweden.

European Bank for Reconstruction and Development (EBRD) (2005), *Transition Report*, London: EBRD.

European Commission (2005), '2005 European Innovation Scoreboard', http://www.trendchart.org/scoreboards/scoreboard2005/docs/EIS2005_database.xls, accessed 11 November 2006.

Honig, B. (1998), 'What Determines Success? Examining the Human, Financial, and Social Capital of Jamaican Microentrepreneurs', *Journal of Business Venturing*, **13** (5), 371–94.

Khanna, T. and K. Palepu (1997), 'Why Focused Strategies May be Wrong for Emerging Markets', *Harvard Business Review*, **75** (4), 41–9.

Kirchhoff, B. (1994), *Entrepreneurship and Dynamic Capitalism*, Westport, CT: Praeger.

Kirov, V. and S. Stoeva (2005), 'Why are Small Enterprises in Bulgaria not Growing?', *Sociological Problems*, **37**, 100–115.

Manev, I.M., B.S. Gyoshev and T.S. Manolova (2005), 'The Role of Human and Social Capital and Entrepreneurial Orientation for Small Business Performance in a Transition Economy', *International Journal of Entrepreneurship and Innovation Management*, **5** (3/4), 298–318.

Miles, M.B. and A.M. Huberman (1984), *Qualitative Data Analysis*, Newbury Park, CA: Sage.

Ministry of Economy and Energy (2005), *Annual Report on the Condition and Development of SMEs in Bulgaria, 2004*, Sofia, Bulgaria: Ministry of Economy and Energy.

Nahapiet, J. and S. Ghoshal (1998), 'Social Capital, Intellectual Capital, and the Organizational Advantage', *Academy of Management Review*, **23** (2), 242–66.

Oliver, C. (1991), 'Strategic Responses to Institutional Processes', *Academy of Management Review*, **16** (1), 145–79.

Peng, M.W. (2003), 'Institutional Transitions and Strategic Choices', *Academy of Management Review*, **28** (2), 275–96.

Peng, M.W. (2001), 'How Entrepreneurs Create Wealth in Transition Economies', *Academy of Management Executive*, **15** (1), 95–110.

Peng, M.W. and P.S. Heath (1996), 'The Growth of the Firm in Planned Economies in Transformation: Institutions, Organizations and Strategic Choice', *Academy of Management Review*, **21** (2), 492–528.

Peng, Y. (2004), 'Kinship Networks and Entrepreneurs in China's Transition Economy', *American Journal of Sociology*, **109** (5), 1045–74.

Puffer, S.M. and D.J. McCarthy (2001), 'Navigating the Hostile Maze: A Framework for Russian Entrepreneurship', *Academy of Management Executive*, **15** (4), 24–38.

Scase, R. (1997), 'The Role of Small Businesses in the Economic Transformation of Eastern Europe: Real but Relatively Unimportant?', *International Small Business Journal*, **16** (1), 13–21.

Smallbone, D. and F. Welter (2001), 'The Distinctiveness of Entrepreneurship in Transition Economies', *Small Business Economics*, **16** (4), 249–62.

Todorov, K. (2001), 'Dinamichnite predpriemachi – Sravnitelen analiz na sustoyanieto i razvitieto im v Bulgaria I Polsha' [Dynamic entrepreneurs: A comparative analysis of their status and development in Bulgaria and Poland], *Narodostopanski Arhiv*, **54** (2), 9–16.

World Bank (2006a), *World Development Indicators 2006*, Washington, DC: The World Bank.

World Bank (2006b), 'Doing Business Indicators', http://www.doingbusiness.org, accessed 10 January 2007.

World Bank (2005), *Building Market Institutions in South Eastern Europe: Comparative Prospects for Investment and Private Sector Development*, Washington, DC: The World Bank.

World Bank (2000), *The Role of SMEs in the Bulgarian Economy*, Sofia, Bulgaria: The World Bank.

Xin, K.R. and J.L. Pearce (1996), 'Guanxi: Connections as Substitutes for Formal Institutional Support', *Academy of Management Journal*, **39** (6), 1641–58.

Yin, R.K. (1993), *Case Study Research (2nd edn)*, Newbury Park, CA: Sage.

4. Regio – a 'learned-global' knowledge company: a case from Estonia

Tõnis Mets

INTRODUCTION

The history of modern entrepreneurship in Estonia started with the transition of the economy after 1991. The disastrous effects of the 1940–91 Soviet heritage become evident if we compare the fate of Estonia to that of its neighbouring country, Finland. In 1940, Estonia and Finland were economically at the same level, but 'according to estimates in 1988, per capita household income was 6 times higher in Finland than in Estonia' (Laar 2004, pp. 4–5). The reason for that was that Estonia had suffered massive Russification and a drop in the share of Estonians in the population from 97 to 60 per cent during the Soviet period (Adamson 2002) – clear proof that the indigenous people had lost control over their own territory and fate. This meant that when Estonia regained independence in 1991, its starting position was far behind that of developed Western countries located in its neighbouring regions around the Baltic Sea.

In 1992, the Estonian government embarked on a liberal economic policy, which is sometimes also referred to as 'shock therapy', and opened the Estonian market to foreign goods and capital. A large-scale campaign of privatization took place, resulting in the collapse of those industries that were not able to adjust to the new economic environment, and leading to a high rate of unemployment for a comparatively long period. This liberal policy supported the inflow of foreign direct investment (FDI), which reached US$4684 per capita (the highest among the transition countries) at the end of 2003 (Varblane 2005). Together, enterprising people and growing FDI have helped to restructure the economy. More recent data show that in 2005 Estonia achieved approximately 60 per cent of the European Union's GDP per capita in purchasing power standards (PPS), and Eurostat predicted its rise to 65 per cent by the end of 2006 (Eurostat 2006).

Yet, despite these rapid economic changes, Estonia cannot be content with the developments that have taken place so far. Productivity and sustainability of growth are still problems. This clearly indicates the need to develop new Estonian industries based on a higher level of added value, and to create more highly qualified and better paid jobs. That implies the need to restructure industry and foster knowledge-intensive production in order to create new products and implement new technologies. A good example of how to move to a knowledge-driven economy is Finland, which has specialized in information and communication technology (ICT), with its flagship company Nokia a global player in the field of mobile technology. But new ICT knowledge is also used as a basis on which to renew its traditional industries of pulp and paper, and engineering (Ylä-Anttila 2006).

Therefore developing new technologies and ICT entrepreneurship have become key issues of economic sustainability in Estonian society. Because of a tiny home market this means internationalization of businesses at their early stage. Estonia has several examples of successful international ICT businesses, such as Skype, Playtech, Microlink and Regio. Unfortunately, in those examples the business models of foreign owners have frequently been more successful than the business conceptions of domestic entrepreneurs: Skype and Playtech, both subsidiaries of foreign companies, became global very quickly. In many cases new knowledge and technology-based companies are 'born global', as innovative SMEs with a global business idea (Luostarinen and Gabrielsson 2004). While Microlink (2005) represents the gradual internationalization model of Estonian corporations, Regio is unique in its globalization process.

The born-global behaviour of young and small technology firms has become a decisive factor in their success. But the born-global concept does not itself explain why and how some hi-tech small and medium-sized enterprises (HSME) become global, while others do not. This chapter aims to study the process of becoming global by looking at the Estonian-owned knowledge-intensive SME Regio. To accomplish this goal, the chapter will cover the following key topics:

(1) A general overview of the environment for knowledge-intensive entrepreneurship, and research and development (R&D) in Estonia.
(2) A development trajectory map for Regio AS, its success story, and analysis of the factors and processes that made its global breakthrough possible.

The chapter deals with these research questions in order to gain a better understanding of the conditions and capabilities contributing to the knowledge economy era: the role of the company founders, the influence of historically inherited knowledge and skills, and the influence of the transitional political, economic and cultural environment around the company on the success of Regio. Even a partial answer to these research questions may be of use to other entrepreneurs, providing some guidelines for economic policy issues related to sustainability within a small transition economy.

CREATING A KNOWLEDGE ECONOMY ENVIRONMENT

The social, economic, cultural and political systems of post-communist countries have undergone considerable changes since the late 1980s. New ways have been opening up for the development of a market economy and democracy in these societies. Generally, the main factors for growth and development are thought to be favourable social and economic circumstances, and the presence of individuals with specific psychological characteristics (Bjerke and Hultman 2002). In the case of Estonia the following questions arise: How well was the society prepared for entrepreneurship in a mental and cultural sense? Which capabilities were inherited from its previous history? And how does the business environment support innovative new businesses?

Researchers have found that the majority of Estonians were never fully convinced of communist ideology (Järä 1999). The particular international factor behind the emergence of Estonian 'self-consciousness' and the early development of entrepreneurship was the fact that from the 1960s many northern Estonian inhabitants were able to watch Finnish television – both because of their geographic proximity and similarity in languages (Elenurm 2004). Consequently, Estonians developed insights and positive expectations of the market economy. Historical memory and other socio-cultural factors were also strong enough in Estonia to lead Estonians to aspire to a restoration of their national and economic independence during the liberalization under Soviet President Gorbachev's *perestroika*, which started in 1986. The concept of Estonia's economic autonomy (IME – an acronym derived from the Estonian words *isemajandav Eesti*) published in September 1987 provoked a wide-ranging discussion and study of market economics among a large number of people (Elenurm 2004). In the same period, the first cooperative and state SMEs as well as international joint ventures were started. Although the IME concept was never completely implemented, it fostered learning, which in turn encouraged the introduction of Estonia's own convertible currency in June 1992 – ten months after the country regained political independence in August 1991.

Another important factor for further development was the economic policy implemented by the new young government which was formed after the first parliamentary elections in 1992. The prime minister, Mart Laar (32 at the time), a professional historian, had studied economics mainly from Friedman: 'I had read only one book on economics, Milton Friedman's *Free to Choose*' (Cato Institute 2006). Since Laar's first period in government, 1992–94, Estonia has implemented a very liberal economic policy. A consequence of following this open economy policy has been Estonia's presence for the past several years in the top ten world economies in terms of economic freedom, varying between fourth and seventh position (Heritage Foundation 2006). This has led to tremendous success in attracting foreign investment, as already mentioned above.

The dynamic development of Estonia was one of the main arguments supporting its accession to the European Union in May 2004. Some general data describing the Estonian entrepreneurial environment and economy are given in Table 4.1.

Changes in GDP are very dynamic and one of the enablers of growth can be seen in the tripling of foreign direct investments (FDI) inflow (Table 4.1). A consequence of this growth is the 4.4 per cent inflation rate. With the 5 per cent TEA index Estonians are no more entrepreneurial than their

Table 4.1   Entrepreneurship environment of Estonia

Indicator	Data (year)	
Population	1 353 600 (2003)	1 346 100 (2005)
GDP per cap at current international US$ (PPP)	13 740 (2004)	17 672 (2006 est.)
GDP growth rate (%)	8.1 (2004)	11.4 (2006)
Unemployment (%)	10.0 (2003)	5.9 (2006)
Inflation (%)	3.0 (2004)	4.4 (2006)
FDI Inflows (as a % of GDP)	8.3 (2004)	21.2 (2005)
Number of companies per 100 inhabitants	6.5 (2005)	8.0 (2007)
Public R&D expenditures (% of GDP)	0.53 (2003)	0.52 (2005)
Business R&D expenditures (% of GDP)	0.28 (2003)	0.42 (2005)
Total entrepreneurial activity (TEA) index[a]	n.a.	5 (2004)

Note: a. TEA index: number of people per 100 adults (between 18 and 64 years of age) who are trying to start their own business or are owners/managers in an active enterprise not older than 42 months (Minniti et al. 2005).

Source: Author's compilation based on Statistical Office of Estonia (2007); IMF (2007); Bank of Estonia (2007); Centre of Registers and Information Systems (2007); Lepane and Kuum (2004).

neighbouring Finns – 5 per cent – or Latvians – 6.6 per cent (Minniti et al. 2005). However, determining the exact number of active entrepreneurs and enterprises is quite complicated because of the dual system of registration of businesses applied by the Commercial Register and by the Tax Department of Estonia; therefore the indicator of 8 companies per 100 inhabitants used in Table 4.1 shows only the data from the Commercial Register.

Rapid economic growth and a positive attitude towards innovation among the Estonian population created a good background for the national innovation system (NIS). Unfortunately, the comparatively high level of ICT implementation is not supported by other technological innovations in industry. Knowledge and technology transfer relations between universities and industries are quite weak, as is mutual interest in cooperation in R&D, which remains low. Since 2000, the annual GDP growth rate in Estonia has been between 7.1 and 11.7 per cent. R&D expenditure closely follows this trend but lags behind the benchmarks of the strategic documents by several years. The benchmark 0.9 per cent for 2003 was achieved as a result of the business sector's growing R&D expenditure in 2005 (Table 4.1). The focus of R&D spending can be evaluated using the ratio of expenditures on fundamental research, applied research and technological development (the R&D ratio). In 2004, spending in the Estonian public–private sector was €50.5 million. The R&D ratio was approximately 3:2:1, and if the business sector was included, it was 3:3:4, with a total R&D spending of €82.7 million. From this we can see that the proportions of financing in Estonia are much more strongly biased towards basic research than in developed countries. Consequently, the NIS is still unbalanced (Mets 2006).

The Swedish researcher Högselius (2005, p. 348) has found that 'the socialist historical heritage, and particular inherited competencies can be used in highly creative ways' in Estonia, and that is exactly what Estonians have done. During the last ten years various innovations have become part and parcel of everyday life. All schools are connected to the internet as a result of the state-run 'Tiger Leap' programme implemented between 1997 and 1999 (Estonian Ministry of Foreign Affairs 2005). Sixty-one per cent of the Estonian population aged between 15–75 could use the internet at the end of 2006, 48 per cent had an electronic ID card, and 75 per cent of internet users used internet banking, while 75.7 per cent submitted their personal tax declarations over the internet (RISO 2006). Wireless internet connections (WiFi), most of them free, are widespread in many regions of the country, totalling 919 areas in a total of 45 000 square kilometres, and have also been installed in local trains as of the end of 2006 (WiFi 2006).

These fast developments became feasible after the collapse of the Soviet regime because of the liberal economic policy of the Estonian government during the twelve-year period before accession to the EU. This policy encouraged both fast transition to a market economy and ICT innovation. The process met with a supportive attitude from the general public. But, despite rapid ICT development, approximately 85 per cent of Estonian manufacturing employees are still working partly in medium and mostly in low-technology industries (Varblane 2005). Traditional Estonian industries must still close a wide gap before they can move on to the knowledge-economy.

INNOVATION AND TECHNOLOGY DEVELOPMENT AT REGIO AS

Story of Regio AS[1]

Regio AS is based in Tartu, a region in South Estonia which has an area of 15 000 km² (30 per cent of country's total area) and a population of approximately 350 000 people (25 per cent of the country's total). The city of Tartu (100 000 inhabitants) differs strongly from the surrounding region by its extremely high concentration of human capital. Tartu is a service centre for the region and a major centre for academic research, higher education and medicine for Estonia as a whole. Founded in 1632, the University of Tartu is the country's largest university with 18 300 students in the academic year 2005/2006 (University of Tartu 2006). In terms of economic development, Tartu appears to counterbalance the industrial north and Tallinn, the financial and administrative capital of Estonia.

Regio has four fields of activity: mapping, geospatial data, geographical information systems (GIS) and mobile positioning (location-based services – LBS). In LBS, Regio is the main subcontractor for Ericsson AB. Not all these competences were part of Regio at its inception. On the contrary, the company acquired these skills during a long period of development. The company's development trajectory is schematically described in Figure 4.1 and the main timeline is given in Table 4.2.

Introductory Period 1988–89: R&D and Postcards

The company was founded as a small state-owned enterprise in the second half of the 1980s, at the time of Gorbachev's *perestroika*. The Ministry of Construction of the Estonian SSR established the company at the initiative of Rivo Noorkõiv (33 at the time), who was also appointed as the first CEO of the R&D firm Regio, or the Regio Firm. Afterwards, when the government of the Estonian SSR in 1989 issued a decree on joint stock

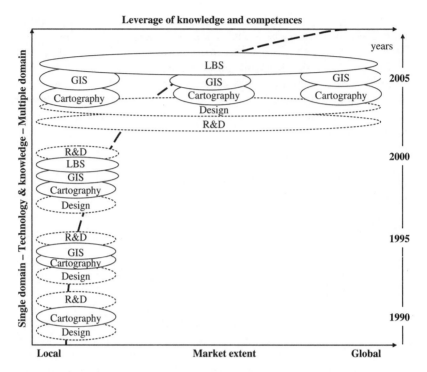

*Figure 4.1   Technology-market learning and development trajectory of
           Regio AS*

companies, the activities were transferred to the private company Regio AS,
founded in 1990 (Table 4.2). At first Regio was based at the Tallinn
Pedagogical University (now Tallinn University), carrying out regional
studies and producing postcards. Regio also published its own working
papers concentrating on questions of demography, nature, regional policy
and so on. 'We participated in creating IME and its regional policy', said
Rivo Noorkõiv in the interview (2006). Today's R&D orientation has its
roots in this early period, and the initial skills in design and printing were also
acquired then. That means that from the very beginning Regio was active in
different knowledge domains that were partly integrated with one another.

Second Period 1989–91: Starting Cartography

As a geography graduate of the University of Tartu (UT), Rivo Noorkõiv
together with Jüri Jagomägi (46), a geographer at the UT, and his son Teet
(19) decided to revive the production of Estonian-language maps and

Table 4.2   Short history and highlights of Regio AS

1988	The Ministry of Construction of the Estonian SSR establishes the state-owned small enterprise Regio Firm, Rivo Noorkõiv (33) – CEO.
1989	Road map of Estonia 1:400 000.
1990	Jüri Jagomägi (47), Rivo Noorkõiv and Madis Michelson establish a private joint stock company Regio AS; Rivo Noorkõiv appointed CEO by the founders (shareholders); the activities are transferred from the state-owned Regio Firm to Regio AS; Regio Firm closed by the new Estonian Government in 1998.
1991	Estonia regains independence.
1992	Sales of Intergraph software.
1993	Teet Jagomägi (23) appointed the CEO; the geo-information system (GIS); the first Estonian sea-map after a 53-year break.
1994	Complete digital map technology using a satellite-based global positioning system (GPS).
1995	Sales of Mapinfo software.
1996	Differential GPS (DGPS) equipment.
1997	Regio produces the first Estonian road-atlas using computer-based technology; CD-Atlas.
1998	The Baltics Small Equity Fund (BSEF) becomes Regio's risk capital partner; Regio is placed sixteenth among Estonian IT companies.
1999	The tender from Ericsson AB for mobile positioning software (MPS); Regio is twelfth among IT companies.
2000	Merge with the Finnish corporation Digital Open Network Environment OY (DONE); spin-off subsidiary Mgine Technologies Estonia OÜ.
2001	Regio admitted into the sales network of Ericsson AB; DONE split into two companies, DONE Solutions and Reach-U Holding.
2002	Bankcruptcy of the parent company Reach-U Solutions; management buy-out of Regio and the trademarks of Reach-U and Mgine Technologies.
2003	The contract with Orange Slovakia to deliver the Reach-U software and LBS.
2004	Global reselling agreement with Ericsson; Estonian Road Atlas – the sixth Estonian bestseller.
2005	Delivery of LBS to Saudi Arabia; contract with Orange Romania; Enterprise of the Year 2005 and Innovator of the Year 2005 Awards.
2006	LBS in Etisalat (United Arab Emirates), Mobily (Saudi Arabia), Dishnet (India), Orange (Slovakia/Romania), EMT (Estonia), Elisa (Finland) and Elisa Vodafone (Estonia); ISO 9001:2000 quality certificate.

globes, starting off with a road-map. Altogether they generated as many as 27 product and business ideas, which were all mostly related to maps (Noorkõiv 2006). It was in this period that the Estonian map production and culture was restored – mainly thanks to Jüri Jagomägi's enthusiasm and experience. The first Estonian road map was completed in 1989 (Püttsepp 1997). It was the first map available to the public for 50 years, as under the Soviet regime all geographical data of the country had been veiled in secrecy.

Third Period 1992–94: Geo-information Systems

In the 1990s, Regio had started to use personal computers and very soon these were used for cartography purposes, that is, the digital data supported the previous paper-based spatial information. Teet Jagomägi trained as a programmer, creating 3D visualization software in Huntsville, Alabama, USA, with Intergraph Corp. from August 1992 until February 1993. On his return from the USA in 1993, Teet Jagomägi, who was still only 23 years old, was appointed CEO of the company (Jagomägi 2005) by the share-holders. Rivo Noorkõiv became a member of the supervisory board. This was a period of specialization in cartography and spatial information. It was also a period of turning separate knowledge and competence domains into a local competitive advantage which led to learning and integration of the new competence – geo-information systems (GIS) in Estonia (Figure 4.1). This period can be called 'the creation of a general knowledge-base'. Regio started to build up its GIS using the satellite-based global positioning system (GPS). In order to finance the investments in computer systems and office, Regio obtained credit from the Maapank bank; both Rivo and Jüri mortgaged their homes for this purpose. In 1993, after a 53-year break, an Estonian sea-map was published again. The move to com-plete digital map technology was finalized in 1994.

Fourth Period 1995–99: Rapid Development and Risk Capital

Regio was the first company in Estonia to invest in differential GPS (DGPS) equipment in 1996. In 1997, the first Estonian road-atlas produced entirely by means of computer-based technology was published. Regio had improved its skills and business profile, having become a software and ICT company as well as a cartography company.

During this period, the company developed its own technologies very quickly, and its annual sales growth reached 51.4 per cent in 1999 (see Figure 4.2). It needed a lot more finance than was available from day-to-day business, in particular in order to break into the international market. The question

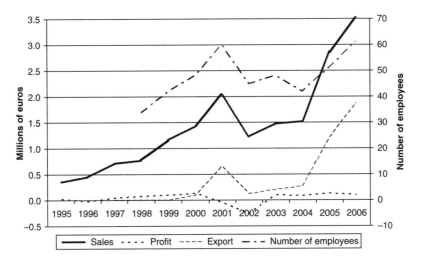

Source: Based on consolidated data from Centre of Registers and Information Systems (2007) and Jagomägi (2007).

Figure 4.2   Sales, export and profit of Regio AS, 1995–2006 (€ millions)

was how to convince big international players that Regio really had advanced knowledge and good development prospects. It was hoped that risk capital would open doors to new networks and new markets, and the American investors Baltics Small Equity Fund became its risk capital partner in 1998.

In 1998, Regio became the biggest GIS software supplier in Estonia. According to the business newspaper *Äripäev* (*Business Daily*), Regio was sixteenth overall in the ranking of Estonian IT companies, and held second place in terms of growth rate profitability.

In 1999, the growth and development of Regio continued. It achieved twelfth place in the overall ranking of Estonian IT companies and it became a member of the Oracle Partner Programme and completed its GIS database covering all the villages of Estonia.

Thanks to its expertise in geo-informatics, Regio won Ericsson AB's tender to develop mobile positioning software (MPS) for the Estonian Rescue Centre. The latter had been using the mobile network service of EMT (an Estonian mobile operator), and Regio's E-112 emergency GSM application became the first mobile positioning system implementation in the world, making it possible to locate mobile phone users. It was Regio's first experience of cooperation with the Swedish company Ericsson AB, the world's leading provider of network infrastructure products to mobile operators (Kodres 2006). This was a period of a new level of technology that combined specific knowledge of different fields, leveraging the existing competences into a new technology competence – location-based services (LBS) (see Figure 4.1).

Despite the first successful cooperation endeavour with Ericsson AB, Regio was still not yet ready to penetrate the international market because of its small size, lack of investment and its Eastern European origins (Tee 2006). The need for additional investment and the lingering low international confidence were the reasons why the owners (shareholders) looked for a strategic partnership and decided to merge with the Finnish corporation Digital Open Network Environment OY (DONE), which was quoted on the Helsinki Stock Exchange. The process was completed in 2000 through a mutual exchange of shares. The Baltic Small Equity Fund realized their Regio shares for cash (Noorkõiv 2006).

Fifth Period 2000–2002: Member of a Listed Company

This period turned out to be shorter than anybody had previously expected. The beginning was promising, as the first MPS was completed, and a spin-off subsidiary Mgine Technologies Estonia OÜ was established to develop positioning software, improving positioning accuracy by between two and eight times.

In October 2001, DONE was split into two companies, DONE Solutions and Reach-U Holding, both quoted on the Helsinki Stock Exchange.

In 2001, the most important business achievement for Regio was its admission into the sales network of Ericsson AB. Mgine Technologies Estonia continued to improve its own software, which was tested in Spain. The MPS product portfolio was sold to DNA, a telecoms operator in Finland (Rozental 2002a). The owners of Regio and Mgine Technologies Estonia decided to incorporate the companies under Regio in November 2001. Regio invested about one million kroons (approximately €64 000) in fixed assets and a little more than three times that amount in product development. The annual growth rate of the consolidated sales of the two companies was more than 40 per cent (see Figure 4.2).

In February 2002, the parent company of Regio went bankrupt. This was the first bankruptcy of a listed internet firm in Finland since the beginning of the twenty-first century (Rozental 2002b). At the time of the merger, the shares of DONE were priced at €4.3, but by the time of the bankruptcy the price had fallen to €0.32. The bankruptcy of the owner, Reach-U Solutions OY, gave Regio managers a chance to repurchase (by management buy-out) the company a year and a half after the merger.

Äripäev wrote that, besides the stocks of Regio, Teet Jagomägi (using his own company Fabian Holdings OÜ – T.M.) bought licences for several technologies developed by Reach-U, which were necessary for Regio to continue its contract with Ericsson AB. 'Reach-U and DONE invested about seven million kroons (approximately €450 000) in the design of new products during the last one and a half years', Jagomägi said, 'we are just now starting to reap the benefits of that, the repurchase happened at exactly the right time' (Rozental 2002b).

Looking back at this period, we can conclude that Regio achieved its main goals in product development, while gaining trust and reaching out to the international market. The backlash from the Reach-U OY bankruptcy, the general slump in the IT sector and the return to independence were not without impact on the business, and in 2002 the sales of Regio fell by 40 per cent (see Figure 4.2). This was the starting point for the current period which is characterized by active investment in product development, market growth and internationalization.

Sixth Period 2002 and Onwards: Independent Again

However, regaining independence did not mean problem-free growth for the company. First, it was necessary to cover the costs of incorporating Mgine Technologies and the losses from the bankruptcy of the parent company. In 2002, Regio suffered the biggest losses in its history (see Figure 4.2), but by the last four months of the year the company had returned to profitability, promising better results for the future and a return to success. In 2003, the first big contract was signed with Orange Slovakia to deliver the Reach-U middle software and LBS (location-based services) package to provide LBS services to their 2.7 million subscribers.

Regio, under the trademark Reach-U, is now officially an associate member of Ericsson Mobility World. In June 2002, Ericsson and Reach-U signed a global reselling agreement which enables Ericsson to offer Reach-U software and mobile applications via its global network. In 2004, Reach-U and Ericsson signed another agreement which officially opens the Ericsson Mobility World sales channel for Reach-U LBS applications (Walmsley 2004).

In February 2005, Regio (Reach-U) delivered mobile positioning to Saudi Arabia, while Orange Romania chose the Reach-U software and LBS package in 2005 to provide LBS solutions for Orange Romania's more than 6 million subscribers, following Reach-U's successful LBS installation with its sister operator Orange Slovakia. The Orange group is one of the largest operators in the world with over 50 million mobile subscribers.

In October 2005, Enterprise Estonia awarded Regio the top 'Enterprise of the Year 2005' Award and the 'Innovator of the Year 2005' Award.[2]

At the end of 2005, Regio employed over 60 highly qualified specialists. Their main development and production unit was located in Tartu, Estonia, while global sales and support was provided through partners (for example, Ericsson) all over the world. Reach-U has held the ISO 9001:2000 quality certificate for software development since 2006.

In January 2006, Reach-U entered another continent by signing a deal with one of the leading operators in North Africa. Now Regio's product portfolio, consisting of LBS software and more than ten LBS applications, is offered to mobile operators around the world. Reach-U's LBS software and applications are currently running commercially on three continents (see Table 4.2).

Regio has been running the biggest internet map server in the Baltic States since 1997. In addition to selling access to its own data, Regio renders geospatial data processing services to its clients, who are mostly utilities and the public sector. This means that Regio is still maintaining the competitiveness of its traditional and new competences.

These latter developments demonstrate that the older competences embedded in the company are integrated with the modern LBS services, and that the good design of Regio's products facilitates good sales promotion. Using the new LBS services requires good maps of the region, and production of well-designed maps has been Regio's strength for more than fifteen years. The competences growing out of each other and complementing each other, such as design and cartography, GIS and LBS, have started to support, that is, to leverage, gross sales in the new markets (see Figure 4.1). This shows that Regio has started to operate on a new level.

KEY FINDINGS

The Role of the Founders in Regio's Business Focus and Culture

Since its inception, Regio's activities have been orientated to R&D, the strong academic background of the first CEO Rivo Noorkõiv and co-founder Jüri Jagomägi (Table 4.3) driving the business idea and initial activities of the company.

Later, the tradition was continued by CEO Teet Jagomägi, who has an MSc in geo-informatics. The R&D focus as well as new knowledge and competence-building have been retained as the main values of the company. Integrating the skills of two generations of university graduates created new competences (which can partly be seen as a family business effect) and developed a multidisciplinary approach to existing competences. The R&D focus of the owner-managers has supported the same

Table 4.3 Profiles of key players

Name	Position in company	Education	Remarks	Date of birth
Rivo Noorkõiv	Founder-shareholder; CEO of Regio 1988–92	MSc geography	Member of Supervisory Board[a] and shareholder until 2000	1955
Jüri Jagomägi	Founder-shareholder; Chief cartographer	MSc geography	Member of Supervisory Board and shareholder until 2000	1943
Eda Jagomägi	Specialist	Geography, University of Tartu	Corrector-editor	1943
Jaan Jagomägi	Project manager; CEO 2002	BSc economics	Member of Supervisory Board 2000–2001	1975
Teet Jagomägi	CEO 1992–2001; since 2003, CEO of Fabian Holding OÜ[b]	MSc geoinformatics	Shareholder until 2000; Member of Supervisory Board 2002	1969

Notes: a. Supervisory Board: the highest governing body of a public limited company in Estonia; b. Sole shareholder of Regio AS after management buy-out in 2002.

aspiration among the employees: five or six of them are currently study-ing for PhDs (Tee 2006). The unique combination of skills has been helpful in finding a strategic partner – Ericsson AB. This has resulted in new LBS products/services based on the competences that have been created.

Until the merger with DONE in 2000, the founders of Regio were also the main shareholders and supervisory board members. After the merger and subsequent bankruptcy of the parent company, Fabian Holdings OÜ, owned by Teet Jagomägi, became the only shareholder (as a result of a management buy-out). The new owner appointed the members of the supervisory board from among distinguished business people of Estonia. The family members, Jüri Jagomägi, Eda Jagomägi and Jaan Jagomägi, remained in the company as specialists in their particular fields. The depart-ment managers were now appointed from among the employees.

Strong mission commitment and active involvement in public life have characterized the leaders of Regio since its inception. This refers to the par-ticipation of the company and its leaders in the creation of the concept of Estonia's economic autonomy (IME) in Soviet times, but also to Jüri Jagomägi's role in restoring the map production culture of newly indepen-dent Estonia. These features, however, have been maintained through the firm's close cooperation with the University of Tartu, while from 1992–96 the former CEO Rivo Noorkõiv held the post of ministerial adviser in the Estonian Government. The current CEO Teet Jagomägi has been elected to Tartu City Council for several terms since 1996.

Historical Inheritance and the Influence of the Environment

The entrepreneurs of Regio owe their attitudes and competences largely to roots that lie deep in Estonia's first independence period (1918–40). But even during Soviet times, Estonians were provided with a good example of normal successful social development by neighbouring market economy countries, especially Finland. Changes in the political environment were very important, since *perestroika* and the end of the Cold War removed the barriers to technology transfer from West to East (Noorkõiv 2006). The most important supportive measure was the government's policy of build-ing up the telecommunication (Högselius 2005) and ICT environment of the country. The development has been dynamic because Estonians 'lack the conservatism and inertia that become more and more characteristic of Western Europe' (ibid., pp. 314–15). New knowledge from the USA enabled Regio to start digital cartography from scratch, unhindered by old systems and practices. In a sense, the latecomer effect supported Regio in starting its own GIS projects with new technology. The economic and social development processes in Estonia and its accession to the European Union in 2004 created more confidence in the business environment.

Besides the general ICT-friendly environment, Regio has used the help of the governmental agency Enterprise Estonia (EE) for technological development and innovation. In the period 2004–05, Regio's training and product development were supported to the tune of approximately €300 000.

A 'Learned-global' Company?

Looking at the highlights of the Regio story, the question arises about the main engine of its internationalization. How much is it the success story of a born(-again) global company, and how much is it a case of (entrepreneurial) learning, knowledge and competence building? What is the importance of the business model, and what is the role played by the business environment and social development?

To answer the first question, Regio can be analysed in two dimensions: the product/service and the market. The product is linked with knowledge, competence and technology, the market with the customer, market share, and the specific needs of the local-global customer on the local-global market (see Figure 4.1). Both of these dimensions are related to the mechanisms connecting and combining their components with each other and as a whole. The first stage in the beginning of the 1990s was the integration of particular knowledge and competence domains into a local competitive advantage, which led to the learning and integration of a new competence – GIS. This is still Regio's leading competence judging by the number of people employed: the department of cartography and geo-informatics provides work for 31 employees, half of the total personnel.

The period of general knowledge-base creation was followed by breakthrough technology or by the creation of the high-level product, LBS (see Figure 4.1). This was a new level of technology combining specific knowledge of different fields; and it became a new technology competence. All these stages featured leverage of knowledge and technology before the market breakthrough happened.

Learning had taken place in the course of the restoration of Estonian map production and culture and individually in the training of software programming and the study of geo-informatics in the USA (by Teet Jagomägi). But there was also learning from experiences from venture capital, the DONE Corporation and the strategic partnership with Ericsson. There were strong organizational learning processes initiated and led by managers to recognize and create new opportunities for business and technology. These became more specific in the business idea, which is the dynamic result of learning and competence-building. All these aspects underlie Regio's high-level offering and globalization.

The market breakthrough happened as a result of the LBS technology fitting into the value chain of the global player Ericsson. It was the starting point for a global market leverage, the speed of which was mainly determined by Ericsson's ability to expand its own mobile network technology; but it also enabled cross-sales of Regio's own products from its earlier portfolio, the GIS and maps which are based on the design and R&D competences developed at the very beginning of the company's existence.

We can conclude that the development process described here has mainly consisted in the growth of knowledge embedded in the people and managers of Regio, while the role of know-how in the product has grown dramatically. It is hard to find one single pure mechanism which has assured Regio's success, as the more powerful ones are combined with simpler ones. But one thing is certain: the capacity for learning and innovation has been inherent in Regio throughout its history. This type of company should best be characterized as 'learned global' rather than a born(-again) global.

CONCLUSIONS

In the fifteen years since regaining independence, Estonia has seen political freedom moving hand-in-hand with self-determination and economic development. Starting with an underdeveloped infrastructure, Estonia has become a rapidly developing, internet-equipped new member state of the European Union. Regio has been at the forefront of Estonia's development and combines the very different and colourful ambitions of Estonian knowledge-intensive entrepreneurship. Regio's story features the founders' and company's self-determination, their desire to seek new ideas, to learn from worldwide experience, to create new ideas and move forward from old ones. It contains a lot of discoveries about technology and the market, as well as unexpected defeats. This is a story full of drama and achievement. But in a way, it is typical of Estonia's development from a Soviet-ruled satellite to independent prosperity. Regio has been an active participant at all stages, from the moment of regaining political freedom to the creation of a modern information- and knowledge-based society in Estonia.

Although Regio is a popular example used to describe the development of technology and strategic thinking among technology entrepreneurs,[3] it remains a rare case in Estonia. In summary, it is a story of how a business started and owned in Estonia achieved an international breakthrough, although the process has not been trouble-free, as is demonstrated by the period as a listed company and the subsequent management buy-back.

Regio is often presented as a family company and a spin-off of the University of Tartu, which is only partly true, as it was started as a small state-owned company in Tallinn, which only later transferred to private ownership and moved its base to Tartu. Its history contains a lot of experience in early capitalist business creation, such as the latecomer's advantage in using new technology, the securing of independence on the domestic market and the drama of internationalization in a merger, the collapse of a partnership, the buy-out of the business again from the bankruptcy assets, and finally, the building up and internationalization of an independent business based on rewarding experiences and know-how. The company has grown together with the public and the business environment of Estonia on a journey from distrust by the developed world to a trusted partnership in the global environment. The success story of Regio shows that even small economies can become global.

The born-global phenomenon becomes especially important because of the limited space for R&D in a small economy. The high-tech small and medium-sized enterprise (HSME) can become global because its business model reaches every customer globally, but there is another way, which is to multiply the business model globally. That means that the HSME is part of the value chain of a global corporation with an existing global business model. The relations between Regio and Ericsson are much closer to the business model of the second type, which can be called the 'model within the model', and Regio itself is a company of the learned-global type, worthy of following by any knowledge-intensive small company.

NOTES

1. Information taken from the company's homepage and annual reports (1999–2005) is not specially referenced.
2. For more information see http://www.eas.ee.
3. See the Henley Management College website: http://www.henleymc.ac.uk/.

REFERENCES

Adamson, A. (2002), *Estonia in 1939–1987*, Estonian Institute: Publications, http://www.einst.ee/publications.html, accessed 6 May 2007.
Bank of Estonia (2007), *Statistical Indicators*, http://www.eestipank.info/frontpage/et/, accessed 6 May 2007.
Bjerke, B. and C. Hultman (2002), *Entrepreneurial Marketing: The Growth of Small Firms in the New Economic Era*, Cheltenham, UK and Northampton, MA, USA: Edward Elgar.

Cato Institute (2006), *Mart Laar's Biography*, http://www.cato.org/special/
friedman/laar/, accessed 6 May 2007.
Centre of Registers and Information Systems (2007), *Statistics*, http://www.eer.ee/,
accessed 6 May 2007.
Elenurm, T. (2004), 'Estonian Perspectives of International Entrepreneurship', in
L.P. Dana (ed.), *Handbook of Research on International Entrepreneurship*,
Cheltenham, UK and Northampton, MA, USA: Edward Elgar, pp. 370–82.
Estonian Ministry of Foreign Affairs (2005), *E-Estonia. Fact Sheet, October
2005*, http://www.vm.ee/estonia/kat_175/pea_175/2972.html, accessed 6 May
2007.
Eurostat (2006), *GDP per Capita in PPS*, http://epp.eurostat.ec.europa.eu/,
accessed 6 March 2007.
Heritage Foundation (2006), *Index of Economic Freedom*, http://www.heritage.
org/research/features/index/, accessed 6 May 2007.
Högselius, P. (2005), *The Dynamics of Innovation in Eastern Europe. Lessons from
Estonia*, Cheltenham, UK and Northampton, MA, USA: Edward Elgar.
IMF (2007), *Global Econ Data*, http://www.econstats.com/weo/C054V011.htm,
accessed 6 May 2007.
Jagomägi, T. (2007), Interview, 28 March, by T. Mets.
Jagomägi, T. (2005), *Teet Jagomägi*, Curriculum Vitae for the seminar of *Äripäev*,
24 March.
Järä, Hanna (1999), 'Dealing with the Past: The Case of Estonia', UPI Working
Papers, No. 15, Helsinki: The Finnish Institute of International Affairs.
Kodres, G. (2006), 'Internationalization of Estonian Technology-Intensive Sector:
The Case of Three Companies', Master's thesis in Entrepreneurship and
Technology Management, Tartu, manuscript.
Laar, M. (2004), 'What We Have Learned in Estonia about Freedom and Growth',
Paper presented at Conference 'A Liberal Agenda for the New Century: A Global
Perspective', 8–9 April, Moscow, http://www.cato.org/events/russianconf2004/
papers/laar.pdf, accessed 6 January 2007.
Lepane, L. and L. Kuum (2004), *Enterprise of Estonian Population*, Tallinn:
Estonian Institute of Economic Research (in Estonian).
Luostarinen, R. and M. Gabrielsson (2004), 'Finnish Perspectives of International
Entrepreneurship', in L.P. Dana (ed.), *Handbook of Research on International
Entrepreneurship*, Cheltenham, UK and Northampton, MA, USA: Edward
Elgar, pp. 383–403.
Mets, T. (2006), 'Creating a Knowledge Transfer Environment: The Case of
Estonian Biotechnology', *Management Research News*, **29** (12), 754–68.
MicroLink (2005), *Closing of Purchase of MicroLink*, Press Release, 16 November,
http://www.microlink.com/ index.php?-6897285, accessed 6 January 2007.
Minniti, M., W. Bygrave and E. Autio (2005), *Global Entrepreneurship Monitor
2005. Executive Report*, www.gemconsortium.org, accessed 6 May 2007.
Noorkõiv, R. (2006), *Interview*, 8 December, by T. Mets.
Püttsepp, J. (1997), 'Teet Jagomägi: olen kasvanud kaartide sees', *Postimees*, 17
September.
RISO (2006), *Statistics*, http://www.riso.ee/et/node/280, accessed 6 May 2007.
Rozental, V. (2002a), 'Teet Jagomägi: Regio tagasi ostmine oli hea tehing', *Äripäev
Online*, 18 March, http://www.aripaev.ee, accessed 6 January 2007.
Rozental, V. (2002b), 'Jagomägi ostis Regio pankrotipesast välja', *Äripäev Online*,
19 March, http://www.aripaev.ee, accessed 6 January 2007.

Statistical Office of Estonia (2007), *Statistical database*, http://www.stat.ee/, accessed 6 March 2007.

Tee, M. (2006), *Interview*, 7 November, by T. Mets.

University of Tartu (2006), *Yearbook*, Tartu.

Varblane, U. (2005), 'Knowledge Based Economy and the Competitiveness of Estonian Economy', Presentation at innovation forum, 'Estonia at a Crossroads', Tallinn, 3–4 November.

Walmsley, K. (2004), *Partner Profile: Reach-U Connects with Success*, 2 December, http://www.ericsson.com/mobilityworld/sub/articles/case_studies/04dec01, accessed 6 January 2007.

WiFi (2006), *WiFi Area*, http://www.wifi.ee/, accessed 6 January 2007.

Ylä-Anttila, P. (2006), 'Finland's Knowledge Economy Today', in C.J. Dahlman, J. Routti and P. Ylä-Anttila (eds), *Finland as a Knowledge Economy: Elements of Success and Lessons Learned*, Washington, DC: World Bank Institute, pp. 9–16.

5. The case of Prohardver, a stop-gap business in Hungary: a real enterprise or a trial test of strength for a young, talented intellectual?

Ágnes Tibor

INTRODUCTION

In Hungary, where after 1956 the centrally-planned system was neither politically nor economically as censorious as in other countries of the region (Csillag and Lengyel 1985), some small businesses existed even before the 'Velvet Revolution' at the end of the 1980s. The old craftsmen who survived the 1950s, 1960s and 1970s differed in almost all points of view from the young ambitious generation of businessmen of the 1980s, but both groups developed within the confines of the socialist system. The entrepreneurs who established their businesses after the great political changes in Eastern Europe may already have been the 'products' of a market-oriented economy, but they continued to reflect elements of the old system. The next two sections of this chapter will present these different types of entrepreneurs as influenced by their particular circumstances. The following section introduces the present political and economical system in Hungary. In the next section, we focus on the case of a young, successful entrepreneur who was formed by the capitalist influences in a market-oriented Hungary. He typifies the new generation of entrepreneurs in the IT sector who tend to be young and creative, to like challenges, and to be full of energy and business ideas.

THE FIRST AND SECOND GENERATIONS OF ENTREPRENEURS IN POST-WAR HUNGARY (1945–81 AND 1982–88)

When the 'modern-day' generation[1] of promising new enterprises emerged in Hungary in the early 1980s, the requisite market, a corresponding regulatory framework and infrastructure were not yet in place (Kun and Tibor 1983; Szirmai 1993). I refer to these enterprises as 'modern-day' enterprises because moonlighting[2] came earlier, namely in the 1960s and 1970s. In agriculture, members of farming cooperatives were allowed to till their household plots. Starting in 1953, a limited number of artisans and privately-owned shops were allowed to operate. However, until the 1980s no one was allowed to own a manufacturing unit or retail outlet of considerable size. In other words, no one could amass a fortune or have employees.

How, then, to differentiate between the small enterprises that emerged in the early 1980s and those that operated before them? These second generation entrepreneurs tended to be individuals with secondary or higher education and they were not solely interested in earning a livelihood for themselves and their families. They sought to offer goods and services that state-owned enterprises failed to offer in the market. These second-generation entrepreneurs were attracted to small business by the new opportunities.

Opportunities arose from economic as well as political causes. As raw material prices rose in the world market in the 1970s, Hungary amassed a considerable national debt. Hungary had adopted a centrally-planned economic system; there were chronic gaps in the supply of goods, and a lot of intellectual potential remained unutilized. There was widespread public dissatisfaction with the assortment of goods available, with living standards and with the opportunities that public undertakings could offer. That tension was defused by the relatively liberal Kádár regime (whose liberalism began in 1958), which introduced novel legal forms of small enterprises.[3] Although allowed only within strict limits, these new entrepreneurial forms enabled those with entrepreneurial spirit to increase their incomes and utilize their intellectual potential. Most of the people who embarked on private enterprise at that time had already engaged in moonlighting.

It would be outside the scope of this chapter to enumerate all the forms of those enterprises, which either operated independently of other public or cooperative undertakings or in symbiosis with them. More people grasped the opportunities offered more quickly than anyone would have predicted. As a rule, the small enterprises then founded had minimal starting capital. Public undertakings and cooperatives could also establish small enterprises – which they did to ensure higher incomes for their employees. At that time a rigid official wage scale prevented any flexibility in wages and salaries.

By 1989–91 when the political regime changed in the other socialist countries, Hungary had about 1 million registered and 871 956 operating enterprises (Kállay et al. 2005),[4] high figures for a country of only 10 million inhabitants. This was a higher level of private business ownership than in Greece (45 businesses for every 1000 inhabitants) or Italy (40 businesses for every 1000 inhabitants) (European Observatory 2003). The new enterprises operated under spartan conditions. They were tolerated, yet they had hardly any access to loans and their interests went unrepresented. In the first period the legal rules set a very low upper limit for the total number of members (10) and employees (30); and small enterprises could only pursue limited areas of activities. Even obtaining a signet (which verifies a business's official status) was a cumbersome procedure; and enterprises were not allowed either to advertise themselves or to have a post box office.

With hindsight, it is clear that the political leaders miscalculated the long-term consequences of opening those initial floodgates (Czako and Vajda 1993; Kuczi et al. 1991; Laky 1992). Many entrepreneurs found loopholes in the system, and as it turned out, some of the small entrepreneurs knew markets abroad better than the big public undertakings and became their competitors internationally. Innovative individuals who were fed up with the indecision of their less creative and sometimes envious superiors often left public undertakings and utilized their inventions in their own enterprise. Many employees became entrepreneurs. Being an entrepreneur even of a small business became a legitimate identity with respected social status.

THE THIRD GENERATION (1988–2000)

The Companies Act was passed in Hungary in autumn 1988. This introduced two new forms of legal businesses: Kft. – a company limited by liability – and rt. – a company limited by shares. In many cases a public undertaking simply assumed the shell of a new legal form and either demerged into smaller units or teamed up to form holding-like clusters. More often than not, the new 'private' owners were the former managers of these public undertakings, their friends, acquaintances and relations as well as former senior Communist Party officials. They formed the first group of the third (post-war) generation of Hungarian entrepreneurs. In some cases they had genuine entrepreneurial skills and managed to foster the requisite political and business ties. They benefited from being in the right place at the right time and using the right opportunity as well as political and 'friendly' connections. Note that we are talking about a period when Hungary still had no law on privatization.[5] Management buyouts (MBOs) and employee share ownership plans (ESOPs) were also applied.

In the latter case, former managers were allotted a greater part of the shares than the regular members. Another option was to sell the public undertaking to foreigners. In some cases entrepreneurs who set up shop in the early 1980s bought public assets, occasionally by benefiting from what was called an 'e-loan' (existence loan[6]). Some of these small business owners are still in business; others entered politics, work as consultants, or live as rich pensioners.

Only in the spring of 1989 did the Hungarian parliament enact a law on privatization, establishing the State Privatization and Asset Management Company (ÁPV Rt.), which became the steward of those public assets that were still left. By that time Hungary was no longer in the Comecon:[7] imported products were pouring in and rivalry between domestic companies was increasing. Large-scale layoffs were the order of the day, both in foreign and Hungarian-owned companies. In 1990–91 the second group of the third generation of entrepreneurs emerged: a large number of 'necessity' entrepreneurs, many of whom were skilled in declining job sectors such as mining, textiles, semi-skilled or unskilled labour and agricultural labour. In addition, a number of necessity entrepreneurs came from the ranks of engineers, teachers, librarians or adult educators who lacked the flexibility to adjust to the dizzying changes of transition and consequently became redundant. Starting their own enterprise might have been the last thing they ever expected to do, but they had no other alternative. Many of them were over 50 but not yet old enough to retire. In general, they spoke no foreign languages and could not sell their labour in the labour market.

There was, in addition, a distinct small group that embarked on enterprise at that time: Hungarians who returned to Hungary after long years in exile. Mostly they did not get their family's old business returned to them, but they were smart and rich enough either to buy it back or to purchase another business.

THE PRESENT SITUATION: FROM 2000 ONWARDS

As for the present situation, laws have now been enacted on bankruptcy and public procurement both of which were previously absent. Standards that are common in Western Europe are now enforced in Hungary. It no longer takes years to obtain registration for enterprises; today it also only takes months to cancel them. Starting on 1 May 2004 (when Hungary became a member of the EU) laws can be read on the homepage of the Hungarian Ministry of Justice and Law Enforcement free of charge. Entrepreneurs, just as any other citizens of Hungary, may obtain loans at nearly forty banks compared with only six banks in the 1980s. Public security is satisfactory; mutual indebtedness among companies has decreased; there is less red tape, and information technology (IT) is much more widely used in public services than fifteen years ago. Company taxes are still high, at 20 per cent of profit in 2006, yet they are tolerable.[8] Inflation dropped from 35 per cent in 1991 to 3.6 per cent in 2005 (Central Statistical Office, 2006).

In addition, the number of people speaking foreign languages has risen both in the public and the private sectors. Employees do not view enterprises with the suspicion that used to be felt in the early 1990s. Unemployment is high, at 7.7 per cent of the working population according to the forecast of the European Commission for 2007 (Népszabadság, 2007), but entrepreneurs can benefit from that: they have a larger pool when they look for employees. As unemployment is high, the cost of labour is relatively low. However, it is not as cheap as in East Asia, which reduces the competitiveness of Hungarian entrepreneurs. The ratio of black (that is untaxed) labour is high, estimated to be approximately 18 per cent of GDP, but again entrepreneurs can benefit from that: they find it easier to hide 'unofficial' employees.

The main sectors of activity for small and medium-sized enterprises (SMEs) in 2003 (by gross value added) were education; repair of motor vehicles; personal and household goods; healthcare and social care; real estate; trade and renting; agriculture and fishing; construction; wholesale and retail trade; hotels and restaurants; manufacturing of furniture, wood, pulp, paper, publishing and printing (Kállay et al. 2005).

The development of science and technology and the implementation of its results are imperative for Hungary, despite the fact that its research and development (R&D) expenditures as a percentage of GDP remain low and amounted to only 0.95 per cent in 2003, less even than the 1 per cent of GDP expended in 1993 (Kállay et al. 2005, p. 211). The government has established many offices, divisions, centres, councils, funds and agencies for stimulating innovation in the economy, but the government's activities are focused on maintaining the status quo rather than on cooperation with or support for innovative activity.

Starting in 1990 there have been many programmes supporting the development of Hungarian small businesses (such as the EU PHARE programme). But nowadays there is only one 'Microcredit' programme. Although different forms of assistance are available, most small entrepreneurs have difficulty accessing them simply because of their inexperience with the specifications and requirements needed by these types of programmes. The current support programmes, together with EU funding, provide the same opportunities for large Hungarian and foreign companies as for Hungarian SMEs.

MÁRTON BALOG AND PROHARDVER LTD

It has taken a decade to aquire a generation of people for whom living under market-economy conditions is a matter of fact, who do not despair if they cannot find a job the day after graduation, and who acknowledge that what they learned yesterday could become obsolete by tomorrow. In short, a generation that understands that it takes time and effort to build a solid livelihood in a market-oriented economy. Márton Balog, Managing Director of Prohardver Ltd, is a member of this generation.

In 1998 Márton and his friend, Dávid Szőts, both 19 years of age, began to buy and sell computer parts. Sometimes they bought inexpensive computers, upgraded them and sold them at a higher price. After two years they started testing computers and computer parts that can be bought in Hungary and making their test results public on the internet, just for fun. No one else had done so in Hungary. Márton and Dávid were both attending university at this time. They regarded their work as a hobby and as an interesting challenge. Both of them were well versed in various internet technologies as they had both had a computer at home since childhood.

Initially they knew little about testing but they learned as they went along. They divided the tasks: Márton wrote the test sheets and found out how to upload the findings to the internet and Dávid did the testing. The first readers were their acquaintances. Then the news spread quickly to the acquaintances of those acquaintances.

Personal Background

Márton received good marks at primary and secondary school even though he did not work hard. He was selective and focused on what he found interesting. Luckily, he was at a secondary school where it was not a requirement to excel in all subjects. The school's headteacher, an ambitious and erudite man, put equal weight on a student's intellectual enrichment and character-building. At this time two favourable aspects of Márton's personality became apparent: his good negotiating skills and his high level of creativity.

As a teenager, Márton and his family spent almost three years in the USA, where his father, a mathematics researcher, was invited to work. Márton developed a good command of English. These years also gave him the opportunity to get acquainted with the highly developed IT sector in the USA.

Back in Hungary, Márton was interested in both economics and IT, but his parents advised him to study economics because they believed that IT would remain a part of his life anyway. After secondary school he entered

the Budapest University of Economics (now called the Corvinus University
of Budapest).

Márton did well at university and found time to write articles on business topics for an economics newspaper called *Figyelő* (*Observer*) in his
spare time. In the second year of university, in addition to studying economics, he enrolled in the Information Science Department of the
Budapest Technical University. Although he only attended technical university for two and a half years, his reputation was good enough to convince many of his fellow students to lend a hand to his and Dávid's IT
enterprise.

Launching the Enterprise

In 2000 a friend of Márton's spent his summer working at the sales
department of a computer wholesaler. The friend thought publishing test
results on the internet would boost sales and asked Márton and Dávid to
conduct the testing. They were more than happy to conduct the assessment
since they believed it would be more reliable and in-depth than what was
available in computer magazines and on the internet at that time. The test
results were published on the internet. The products they tested were
mainly borrowed from the wholesaler and Márton and Dávid were thrilled
to get the chance to experiment with some expensive computers. In terms
of employment status, Márton and Dávid were the only permanent
members of the testing staff though they were not paid any wages.

In that same year 2000 Márton and Dávid decided to turn their hobby
into an enterprise. They registered Prohardver as a Kft. (Ltd). By this time,
they had earned name recognition for their tests on the internet. More and
more wholesalers and, for the first time, producers, approached them
requesting tests. This type of business was very appealing for Márton and
Dávid because it used their IT skills and it required little investment since
they did not have to buy either the computers to be tested or the instruments to be used in the tests.

In founding their limited company they included their computer-testing
internet portal as a non-cash contribution in the corporate assets. The
stakes of the limited company were divided in the following manner:
Márton and Dávid held 45 per cent each and two others held 5 per cent
each. One of the latter two is presently the firm's accountant, the other
doesn't work for the firm any more.

Márton and Dávid worked ten to twelve hours a day. In 2002 their internet portal had only about 500 daily visitors. At this time an acquaintance
helped them get some software-related assignments from an internet service
provider (ISP), and the ISP gave them a server, which provided them with

the opportunity to upload any materials they wanted on the internet. As a rule, they used barter trade instead of cash when obtaining new hardware. For two and a half years, until 2003, they had no office of their own. The computers were assembled, tested and disassembled in Dávid's parents' garage.

They officially converted their hobby into a business when they realized that there were people who were ready to pay for their services. First they approached only a couple of wholesalers with the offer to test some of their products and publish the test results on the internet free of charge. Over time they approached additional wholesalers. When their readers numbered in the hundreds, including employees of IT firms, more and more wholesalers were responsive. Then they officially established their firm and began charging a fee for their service on the grounds that the test results also served as advertisement. The price rose from HUF 25 000 (€100) to HUF 100 000 (€400) per month for a test-order company client. In 2002 the turnover was 3 million HUF (€12 000).

Both Márton and Dávid realized it was important to increase their numbers of readers. They contacted an acquaintance who knew someone at Index, one of Hungary's most popular webzines. They were able to convince Index to include their service in Index's portal free of charge. That move proved to be a breakthrough: the number of visitors to their homepage soared. At that time, Prohardver attracted three main types of customers. (1) Producers and wholesalers, both of whom lacked first-hand information about the market in terms of their rivals or their customer needs. Prohardver filled this gap by providing objective information about products on the market. (2) Do-it-yourselfers: especially those searching for new computer modules and computer configurations. (3) Corporate buyers of IT products.

Márton and Dávid have made it a point to keep abreast of the latest technological developments while keeping expenses low. In 2003 they attended CEBIT[9] in Hanover – on a shoestring. They convinced an acquaintance to give them a lift there and back and only spent one day at CEBIT in order to save on hotel costs. At the fair they visited the stands of minor computer parts manufacturers from Taiwan and sought to establish contacts.

Prohardver's Main Activities

Testing computer parts is straightforward work. On average four units are tested weekly, and the results are immediately published on the internet. Prohardver's internet portal is updated with ten news items per hour, and almost all items are archived. Unlike the majority of other dot-coms and brick-and-mortar firms, they receive advertisements by networking with wholesalers and, less often, producers, rather than through advertising agencies. Prohardver has been able to hire excellent experts. Today the enterprise also owns testing instruments to corroborate assessments.

Approximately 90 per cent of their income is derived from advertisements. The Prohardver portal carries paid advertisements in the form of banners. But they never publish promotional articles on the test pages (although some competitors do).

In 2005, they were visited by 25 000 persons daily and boasted approximately 70 000 registered forum members. Prohardver has long since grown out of the garage. In 2002 they moved the enterprise to a flat rented from the aunt of a staff member and in January 2005 the enterprise moved to offices in a neighbourhood full of computer wholesalers (their main clients) near the Pest entrance of Árpád Bridge in Budapest.

Gradual Growth

The enterprise's expansion is always based on a new idea, and it usually takes a few months to be realized. When testing is extended to a new category of products, a new sub-page is launched. For example: IT news Hungary (http://www.it.news.hu), a portal with news for businesses, was launched in 2004. Geared to middle management readers, it covers news and new tendencies in the computer industry.

Using their existing expertise, Prohardver has formed an agreement with Mobilarena, a portal that carries test results and news about mobile phones. Prohardver provides the technical basis for an internet presence and secures advertisers while Mobilarena supplies the content. The two-member staff of Mobilarena receive a total monthly salary of HUF 250 000 (€1000). But when Mobilarena's revenue rises above HUF 500 000 (€2000) per month, half of the remainder is transferred to Prohardver as payment for use of Prohardver's name.

Since regular readers of Prohardver are IT aficionados, in 2005 Prohardver began selling IT services such as ADSL[10] access to the internet. The core activity is still the Prohardver test portal, which is the market leader in Hungary. However, the main test portal is not the only one that generates revenue: the IT news portal (http://www.it.news.hu) fetches HUF 6 000 000 (€24 000) in sales yearly. The enterprise is considering launching a portal on entertainment electronics but only if it will be profitable. Today Prohardver is the biggest and best-known dot-com technical media portfolio in Hungary.

Always seeking diversification and always optimistic about the prospects of e-commerce, Márton is planning to launch two more portals: one carrying ads and another serving as a marketplace. The latter has won a grant of twenty million HUF (€8000) under the Hungarian First National Development Plan. The sum will be paid by the Ministry of Economy and Transport under the European Union-sponsored Economic Competitiveness Operative Programme.

Division of Labour

In 2006 Prohardver had ten employees, with all but one working full-time. New staff members are often hired through the website. Education is not important, what matters is the way in which potential employees solve their first assignments. In addition, they have to be highly motivated and committed. Interestingly, one of the newcomers used to be the manager of a rival internet portal. He joined Prohardver in the hope of obtaining a higher sense of accomplishment. Márton is the managing director: his tasks include management, charting out new directions for the enterprise, devising the design of the portal and the arrangement of the news items, in addition to coordination, business negotiations, keeping in touch with clients, selling advertising space and acting as the forum's moderator for the portal. He has two immediate subordinates: an editor in chief – who is also his deputy – and an advertising organizer. The editor in chief, Eva Horváth, the only woman on the staff, joined the enterprise a year ago. She writes the news and edits articles written by two other staff members. Before joining the enterprise, she worked for computer wholesalers. She has extensive field experience in Hungary, in addition to spending two years in the United States. She is a born organizer and is also in charge of purchases and logistics; she coordinates testing, liaises with partners and clients, and eases Márton's burden. Dávid and two other staff members are in charge of testing the computer components. One of the staff members liaises with advertising agencies. In an increasing number of cases producers approach Prohardver to offer computers and parts for testing and often such relationship involves the placement of advertisements. The staff of the IT news portal (http://www.it.news.hu) includes two journalist-editors and so does that of Mobilarena. A few months ago a young man was hired on a part-time basis, who will do programming to ease Márton's workload. It is difficult to show a clear organizational chart, because everybody helps out wherever needed.

Sales, Costs and Profits

Each staff member, including Dávid, earns a net wage of HUF 150 000 (€600) per month when they fulfil their job duties, while Márton earns HUF 200 000 (€800) per month. That is on a par with average monthly salaries in Hungary. At the end of each month Márton counts the number of articles written by individual staff members and assesses what other work they have done. (There is a computer programme to assist him in that assessment.) Only the four owners receive shares in proportion to their ownership stake. The enterprise is not cost-intensive because the work is highly knowledge- and work-intensive.

Sales as well as profits have been increasing for years. As early as 2002, sales stood at HUF 3 million (€12000); in 2003 at HUF 15 million (€60000); in 2004 at HUF 40 million (€160000) and in 2005 at over 60 million (€240000). As the enterprise's costs are low and many early transactions were barter trade agreements, profits have been high, averaging about half of total sales.[11] Most of the costs are comprised of rent and personnel payments. It usually takes six months to generate funds for the realization of a new idea. The greater part of the profits is drawn as dividends, that is, they are not reinvested.

Assistance, Business Partners and Rivals

The suppliers of Prohardver are both domestic and foreign wholesalers, and Hungarian producers. These firms contact the enterprise directly and offer products for testing. Prohardver's customers place advertisements on any of Prohardver's internet pages. The enterprise does not maintain close contacts with any of its competitors. It only deals with products that are covered on its pages. It rarely applies for state grants and does not engage in lobbying.[12] The enterprise has not taken any loans from banks or other financial institutions since there has been no need to do so. It has not asked for the assistance of any consulting firms because it knows the market better than they do. It has not sought assistance in drawing up business plans because it has never written any. Accounting is done by one of the minority owners. Extension training is done voluntarily on a day-to-day basis, as part of work. As for skills in marketing, management and negotiations, the enterprise relies on Márton's intrinsic talent. Information is collected from the internet and then passed on in-house and, through its website (http://www.it.news.hu), to the public, including competitors. They do not have a company lawyer on staff, but could find a corporate legal adviser among their acquaintances. So far, efforts have been made to settle differences with competitors amicably through compromises. Some producers have threatened to take them to court for their negative test results, which could eventually convince them to hire a legal adviser. 'If we are taken to court by a multinational company', says Márton, 'we have little chance of winning.'

In terms of strategic planning, Márton has the task of monitoring the market, the state of the economy and the behaviour of competitors. He regularly comes up with proposals on how the enterprise should adjust to new developments. For example, since tax hikes and other economic restrictions are expected in Hungary, the number of wholesalers is likely to decrease. By contrast, e-commerce is on the rise, which means the players that remain in business are expected to place more advertisements with Prohardver than in the past. Prohardver cultivates lively professional relations with other companies since networking is crucial for all small enterprises. Prohardver's partners include the Hungarian Index (http://www.index.hu), the Hungarian subsidiary of the German publisher Vogel Burda (http://www.vogelburda.hu) and a Taiwanese advertising agency, which is well-placed to attract the attention of producers in Taiwan. Though the Taiwanese advertising agency has not yet arranged any advertisements for Prohardver, year by year, under a barter agreement, it enables Prohardver's representatives to visit the Computex exhibition in Taiwan, where they can meet with local Taiwanese producers.

Future Prospects

Conditions have become somewhat harsher recently for Prohardver. Fewer computer users wish to buy a new computer every second year and at the same time fewer computer users are continuously upgrading their computer systems.

There have been other changes that are even more important. The market has become more consolidated. Wholesalers have become more specialized. Minor computer vendors have gone bankrupt. Only about a dozen wholesalers have remained, and they are so well known among potential buyers that they do not need to advertise themselves regularly. Should they decide to advertise themselves at all, they tend to turn to companies that are bigger than Prohardver. In this sense, Prohardver caters to a specific market niche; people who are not involved with IT are unlikely to visit its internet pages. Consequently, the traders and producers often place their advertisements about new products in the technical news sections of popular general-purpose webzines because they hope to reach a wider audience. Although Prohardver was the first in its field and is operating at high standards, a number of competitors have emerged. An example is the Hungarian IT portal (http://www.HWSW.hu). Other competitors include off-line IT magazines such as: *IDG*, *Game Star* and *Számítástechnika* (*Computer Science*), as well as major on-line magazines, irrespective of their specialization. Further potential competitors include multinational companies that are also involved in publishing test results: Sanoma, Ringier, T-Online and Origo, which might decide to buy or create a similar internet portal at any time.

Prohardver is set up as a cluster of small units because Márton does not wish to manage an enterprise that has more than thirty employees. He does not want to work more than 10 to 12 hours a day or to go to work in a dark suit. Márton does not make long-term plans for several reasons. 'Long-term plans do not work in this market', he says. When a good idea comes up, one that promises to be profitable, it needs to be realized within a short time. Each new project is expected to become self-sustaining within a very short period of time. As they have dozens of new ideas weekly, it does not seem to be necessary to save money over a long period to realize a major new project.

In thinking about diversification, foreign markets have been considered. There was a proposal to make an English-language version of the test portal, but there would be too many rivals, and it would be difficult to attract advertisements. Another proposal was to enter another new European Union accession country's market but there they would have neither field experience nor connections, plus there would a language barrier. Thus, diversifying into another country is not on the agenda for the time being. However, suppliers often ask Prohardver to have their test results translated into a foreign language. About one-third of the enterprise's annual sales come from non-resident advertisers.

Márton is now 26 years old and no longer attends university. He has not found time in the last three years to write his MSc diploma thesis although he plans to complete and defend his Master's thesis before the end of 2007. That is just one of the reasons why he devotes less time to Prohardver than before. There are many other things that interest him, which means he does not want the enterprise to absorb all his attention. Even if he moves to another area, perhaps acting as an entrepreneur at another enterprise, he does not intend to sever relations with Prohardver. He plans to devote two days per month at Prohardver if he enters another field. In that case he would act as an investor. After all, he would remain a co-owner and as such, he needs to know the workings of his investment.

Márton and Dávid began building the internet portal for testing hardware components at the right time. It would not be worth launching such an enterprise today, given the present market conditions. 'We are in a monopoly position', he says, 'and the big companies, like Sanoma, do not find it a good idea to launch an internet portal similar to Prohardver in Hungary's shrinking market. Although the computer-engineering market is not growing at the same pace as it did in previous decades, Prohardver has a reading audience of about two hundred thousand people. There seems to be an opportunity to offer new portals for our readers – in the same way as it happened over the past three years ... It gives reason for optimism', Márton continues, 'that some paper-based magazines are interested in being on the internet and enter into close cooperation with Prohardver.'

Márton has been a successful entrepreneur because he is good at his trade, that is, information technology, as well as a committed business owner. He is responsive to the enterprise's economic, political and social environment; he has the requisite flexibility and, when necessary, the ability to make rapid decisions. He is committed now to Prohardver and will remain so until he finds something else to do. After all, he is young and is not preoccupied either by money or by IT.

The strengths and weaknesses of Prohardver at the end of 2006 and the beginning of 2007 can be summarized as follows. In terms of strengths, first and foremost, Prohardver's corporate name is well known. Their portals and subportals are popular. Because visitors are requested to register when they visit the portals, a user database can be created that can focus further marketing activities. In addition, Prohardver has good relations with a wide range of players in the internet community, which forms an excellent basis for launching further activities.

Weaknesses arise from the fact that the e-marketplace is quite new in Hungary, with only a few customers and users. Many potential clients distrust such firms, fearing fraud. Moreover, weaknesses in terms of future development of the firm are related to the growth intentions of the entrepreneur. Although Márton Balog, with some suitable colleagues, would be capable of turning his enterprise into a large and prosperous company, it is not sure that they will do it. The first obstacle is Márton's personality. Though he is prepared to run certain risks, is a good organizer, is driven to realize profits from his enterprise, keeps innovating his enterprise and utilizes good opportunities, although he is open and creative and has the ability to invigorate others, he is not really motivated to realize profits and is not interested in capital accumulation – even if by doing so he could lay the foundations for his enterprise for life. Márton is young and would like to have experiences of other types. He does not have a strategic approach to his enterprise because he doubts whether it is where he wishes to remain for the long term.

The second obstacle is that competing Hungarian public undertakings and foreign multinational-owned undertakings use (and misuse) their special connections with those wielding political power, monopoly positions, legal loopholes and hard-to-access information. When it comes to competition with them, even the most talented small entrepreneur is in a handicapped position.

CONCLUSION

Hungary is unlike other transition countries because it has had three different generations of entrepreneurs. The first generation consists of the old craftsmen and shopkeepers, who work using outdated technology in small, dark workshops in traditional districts of the towns or parts of the village, and earn small amounts of money. The second generation consists of five different groups (also compare Dallago 1997; Stark 1992). (1) Former cadres, who are better educated than the first group and have good personal and business connections with former colleagues and present-day politicians. They are well informed and have money for development of the business, but lack the interest and the skills for developing their newly acquired business. Instead they were mainly interested in rent-seeking activities, using their profits to live luxuriously. (2) Former exiles, who bought their old family business or other businesses. (3) Small entrepreneurs, who decided to develop their own business from personal savings made from their business in the 1980s. (4) The self-employed, who did not want to or could not continue working for their employers. They tend to enjoy having their own business and can sustain themselves or their whole family. (5) The must-be entrepreneurs, who could not find any other job (employment), because they do not speak foreign languages or are not able to manage a business, or are too old to build up market connections or start to learn an independent business – those who would otherwise be unemployed.

Márton, the 'hero' of our case study, is an example of the third generation of entrepreneurs. He has grown up under free-market conditions, is educated, talented, can manage a small business successfully, and could probably further develop his business, if he wanted to.

The transition process offered opportunities for everybody who wanted to establish a business. However the conditions were not the same for different groups of entrepreneurs. As the privatization of public enterprises is almost complete, a new generation is growing up characterized by people accustomed to more or less stable market conditions. Therefore it can be expected that in the long run (experts estimate 15 up to 20 years) the characteristics of the Hungarian SME sector will converge with those in the old EU countries.

NOTES

1. 'Generation' in this case is my own phrase.
2. Moonlighting in this chapter refers to work (manufacturing or service) on the side, utilizing resources available at the workplace in public undertakings that are not reported to the tax authority.
3. Actually, reform-minded junior politicians elaborated the package and by the time the senior decision-makers recognized the consequences, it could not be undone.
4. The number of Hungarian registered enterprises is cited from the Central Statistical Office, the number of operating ones from the Hungarian Tax Office.
5. An example of how a chief executive officer (CEO) of a public undertaking could become its owner: the CEO writes off the assets of the public undertaking and sells them to his acquaintance who then resells them back to him.

6. This was a special loan whereby Hungarians who already had a certain amount of assets (this changed from time to time) could buy a stake in a Hungarian public undertaking.
7. Comecon: the Soviet-led economic alliance of Communist countries until 1989.
8. The company tax rate was 40 per cent of profit in 1992.
9. CEBIT is the world's largest trade show for communication technology.
10. ADSL: Asymmetric Digital Subscriber Line – it allows for a quicker digital transmission than the traditional providers.
11. An example of such barter deals: the five servers of the enterprise are from five companies which get advertising space on Prohardver's portal in exchange.
12. Though when it applied for the above-mentioned European Union-sponsored grant, it pulled some strings at ministerial levels.

REFERENCES

Central Statistical Office (2006), *Yearbook of the Central Statistical Office*, Budapest.

Csillag, István and László Lengyel (1985), *Vállalkozás, állam, társadalom* (Enterprise, State, Society), Budapest: Közgazdasági és Jogi Könyvkiadó.

Czakó, Ágnes and Ágnes Vajda (1993), *Kis- és középvállalkozók'* (Small and Medium Entrepreneurs), Budapest: MVA Kutatási Füzetek 2.

Dallago, Bruno (1997), 'The Economic System, Transition and Opportunities for Entrepreneurship', in: OECD/LEED (eds), *Entrepreneurship and SMEs in Transition Economies*, Paris: OECD, pp. 103–24.

European Observatory (2003), *SMEs in Europe 2003*, Brussels: Enterprise Directorate.

Kállay, László, Kálmán Kőhegyi, Eszter Kissné Kovács and Ludmilla Maszlag (2005), *A kis-és középvállalkozások helyzete. Éves jelentés 2003–2004* (State of Small and Medium-Sized Business in Hungary), Budapest: Ministry of Economics and Transport.

Kuczi, Tibor, Beáta Nagy, György Lengyel and Ágnes Vajda (1991), 'Vállalkozók és potenciális vállalkozók' (Entrepreneurs and Potential Entrepreneurs), Budapest: Budapesti Közgazdaságtudományi Egyetem, manuscript.

Kun, Tibor and Ágnes Tibor (1983), *Vállalkozók zsebkönyve* (Pocketbook for Entrepreneurs), Budapest: Alkotó Ifjúság Egyesülés.

Laky, Teréz (1992), *Small and Medium-Size Enterprises in Hungary: Report for the European Commission*, Budapest: Institute for Labour Studies.

Népszabadság (2007), 10 March.

Prohardver – website of the Ministry of Informatics and Telecommunications www.itkht.hu/engine.aspx?page=showcontent=nyertes, accessed in 2005.

Stark, David (1992), 'Path Dependence and Privatization Strategies in East Central Europe', *East European Politics and Societies*, **6**(1), 17–54.

Szirmai, Péter (ed.) (1993), *Kisvállalkozások helyzete és fejlesztésük feladatai* (Situation of Small Enterprises and How to develop them), MVA Vállalkozáskutatási Füzetek No 3. Published by SME Group of Budapest University of Economic Sciences.

6. Our future looks even more promising! The case of Libra Holding in Lithuania

Ruta Aidis

6.1 INTRODUCTION

I arrive on time at the Holiday Inn in Vilnius for my meeting with Tomas Juška, CEO of Libra Holding, the largest wood-processing company in Lithuania. He is already waiting for me, a bluetooth in his ear and tapping away on his laptop. At 38 years of age, Tomas's entrepreneurial experiences illustrate a new breed of entrepreneurs in Lithuania, those who grew up under Soviet control but were well positioned to pursue the opportunities that developed during the initial stages of independent Lithuania's emerging market economy.

A number of successful high-tech companies have developed in the post-transitional environment in Lithuania. As in other formerly centrally-planned economies, the legacy of high investments in human capital, especially in the fields of science and engineering, have provided fertile ground for successful companies such as Fermentas and Sicor Biotech to take root and flourish in Lithuania. These types of firms tend to be synonymous with innovation. However, this case study chooses to focus on another type of innovation that embodies the essence of entrepreneurial opportunities as they develop in chaotic 'anything goes' transitional environments where even young, inexperienced college students can set up a successful international manufacturing company in a matter of years. The Libra Holding case also highlights the fact that other areas of innovation can be as important as product development. The company's philosophy and strong leadership provide crucial support for business success and excellence.

This chapter is structured as follows. Section 6.2 provides a brief background description of the Lithuanian context and Section 6.3 highlights the characteristics of private sector development in Lithuania. Section 6.4 focuses on the Libra Holding case study. The key findings of the case study are discussed in Section 6.5 and the chapter concludes in Section 6.6.

6.2 LITHUANIA

Lithuania has an area of 67 000 km^2 and is located on the Baltic Sea. It is bordered by Latvia on the north, Poland on the south, Russia's Kaliningrad enclave on the west and Belarus on the east. After a period of independence, during World War II Lithuania was illegally annexed into the Soviet Union in June 1940. Following a brief revolt and occupation by Nazi forces, Lithuania was re-annexed into the Soviet Union in 1944. This Soviet occupation lasted for almost five decades.

In the late 1980s, non-violent Lithuanian resistance gained momentum and prevailed in spite of Moscow's provocations. On 11 March 1990, Lithuania was the first Soviet republic to declare its independence from the Soviet Union. However, Lithuania's independence was only internationally recognized more than a year later in August–September 1991[1] causing much economic and social damage.[2] By the end of 1992, Lithuania's secession from the Soviet Union was formally completed (marked by the removal of all foreign[3] troops from Lithuanian soil) at which time it embarked on an ambitious stabilization and reform programme supported by the International Monetary Fund (IMF) and the World Bank (WB).[4]

Lithuania has approximately 3.4 million inhabitants (EBRD 2005). In comparison to the other former Soviet republics, Lithuania's economic performance has been quite good. However, the transition process has not been easy for most of Lithuania's inhabitants. In the early 1990s inflation rates skyrocketed, purchasing power fell dramatically and unemployment levels continued to increase. In 1994, Lithuania's gross domestic product (GDP) amounted to only 54 per cent of its former amount in 1989. Even by 2004, GDP was only 89 per cent of its pre-transition 1990 level[5] (EBRD 2005). In comparison with the eight other new EU member countries shown in Table 6.1, Lithuania's performance falls in the middle range: not exhibiting very high levels of FDI inflows or high unemployment but maintaining low inflation.

The percentage of GDP in Lithuania generated by the private sector has been steadily increasing since 2002 and made up 75 per cent of GDP in 2005. The growth of the private sector demonstrates Lithuania's commitment to privatization and the development of a free-market economy. The rapid decline in the importance of the agriculture sector (as a percentage of GDP) has also been a positive development. In 1990 the agricultural sector contributed more than 27 per cent of GDP whereas in 2004, its

Table 6.1 Comparative statistics of the eight new Eastern European EU member countries

	Czech R.	Estonia	Hungary	Latvia	Lithuania	Poland	Slovak R.	Slovenia
Population in millions	10.2	1.4	10.1	2.3	3.4	38.2	5.4	2
Area ('000 sq. km)	78.9	45	93	64.5	67	313.9	49	20.5
GDP (in billion US$ 2004)	107	11.2	100.3	13.5	22.3	241.8	41.1	32.2
GDP per cap in 2004 at current international US$ (PPP)	19 311	13 740	16 596	11 962	12 994	12 876	14 549	20 853
Private sector share in GDP in 2005 (%)	80	80	80	70	75	75	80	65
Inflation 2005 estimation (%)	2	3.9	3.8	6.4	2.8	2.2	2.4	2.5
Unemployment rate (UNECE 2003) (%)	7.8	10.1	5.8	10.5	12.7	19.2	17.1	6.5
FDI inflows 2004 (as a % of GDP)	3.7	7	3.6	4	2.3	2	1	3.3
Est. level of real GDP in 2004	114	112	120	90	89	142	121	126

Source: EBRD Transition Report (2005); UNECE for unemployment rates (http://www.unece.org).

contribution had shrunk to less than 5.2 per cent (EBRD 2005). Subsequently, the importance of the service sector in GDP has been increasing and by 2000 contributed close to 60 per cent of GDP (ibid.).

In Lithuania as elsewhere in the former Soviet bloc transition countries, economic reform heavily emphasized the privatization of state-owned enterprises and the needs of the state-owned sector. In general, the focus was on privatization and reform rather than on the development of an entrepreneurial class.[6] Acs and Audretsch (1993) identify one of the main challenges confronting Central and European countries as the development of entrepreneurship in order to achieve a more balanced industrial sector. New firms tend to be better at adapting to the radical switch from a centrally-planned economy to new market conditions which necessitate new resource combinations and innovation. As Kontorovich (1997) observed there are three main actors on stage in post-centrally-planned economies: communist-era firms, domestic entrepreneurs and foreigners. While privatized enterprises are frequently struggling with reform and restructuring and foreigners are grappling with limited information and insight, the new domestic entrepreneurs emerge as heroes of the transformation. Taking this into consideration, entrepreneurship and especially small and medium-sized enterprises (SMEs) play an important role in Lithuania's future economic development.

6.3 PRIVATE ENTERPRISE DEVELOPMENT

Though private enterprise was severely restricted in Lithuania under Soviet rule, private enterprise and small and medium-sized farm production dominated the economy in pre-Soviet Lithuania before World War II. Then again in the early 1990s, following Lithuania's post-Soviet experience, private enterprise reappeared on the economic landscape in record numbers. From 1993–95 the numbers of private enterprises in all size categories continued to increase steadily. As Table 6.2 shows, the most rapid growth took place in the smallest size category (fewer than 5 employees and 5–19 workers).[7]

However the period from 1999 to 2000 has been characterized by decreasing numbers of registered SMEs. At the beginning of 1999 there were 81 600 registered[8] SMEs but by the end of 2000 there were only 52 000 registered SMEs (Lithuanian Development Agency for Small and Medium-sized Enterprises (SMEDA) 2002[9]). The main factors influencing this rapid decrease seem to be both internal changes and external economic shocks. Internal changes included increased labour costs (for hiring employees), additional taxation, additional bureaucratic barriers, increased competition

Table 6.2   The number of functioning registered enterprises in Lithuania

	1993	1994	1995
Functioning enterprises	33 067	47 650	63 241
Fewer than 5 workers	24 214	35 865	48 321
5–19 workers	5123	7100	9151
20–199 workers	3348	4225	5192
200+ workers	382	460	577

Source: UNDP (1997).

from large chain stores (especially for trade-related businesses) and low consumer demand. External shocks included both the Russian rouble crisis (August 1998) and an increasingly unfavourable litas-euro exchange rate. The Lithuanian Human Development Report (UNDP 1999) noted that the Russian crisis was hardest on small businesses that were involved in trade with Russia. In addition, the litas was tied to the US dollar and the increasing value of the US dollar and the decreasing value of the euro resulted in Lithuania's exports being less competitive and made it more difficult for Lithuanian SMEs to engage in profitable export activities. However, a simplification of the regulations for de-registering inactive businesses in 2000 may have influenced the apparently large decline in private businesses from 1999 to 2000.

As Lithuania's free-market economy stabilizes and matures, the density of SMEs remains low. At the end of 2005, there were 56 428 functioning SMEs in Lithuania which translates into an SME density of 15.6 active SMEs per thousand inhabitants (SMEDA 2006). This is quite low when compared to the average density of 50 SMEs per thousand inhabitants in the rest of the EU. Approximately 75 per cent of all Lithuanian SMEs are micro enterprises, having fewer than 10 employees. In terms of sectors, most SMEs are engaged either in trading activities (38 per cent) or other services (24 per cent) while 15 per cent are active in industry, 7 per cent in construction and 16 per cent in other activities. The majority of active SMEs in Lithuania are incorporated (54.5 per cent) (ibid.).

6.4   LIBRA HOLDING: THE BUSINESS IDEA AND TAKE-OFF OF THE FIRM

The case study of Libra Holding provides an excellent illustration of the initial opportunities that were available for entrepreneurial individuals in the early 1990s in Lithuania. Though it is not a high-tech company, Libra

Holding displays a high level of innovativeness through its business operations as well as its unconventional business philosophy. In order to understand the development of Libra Holding, it is important to understand the circumstances that led to its creation as well as the characteristics and background of its founders. The section below outlines these issues using the current CEO of Libra Holding, Tomas Juška, as the focal point.

Tomas Juška was born in 1968 in the town of Kėdainiai but grew up in rural northeastern Lithuania. During his youth he was aware of the injustice and inequality that occurred in rural areas: 'Some people seemed to work very hard but still had a hard time surviving.' This was one of the main motivations for Tomas's choice to study manufacturing economics[10] at Vilnius University. Not long after Tomas began his studies at the university, the transition process in Lithuania began and radically influenced Tomas's future choices. In 1990, attracted by these new market developments, Tomas and four friends (three of whom roomed with him and one who lived across the hall) decided to volunteer at the newly established Free Market Institute.[11] The complete novelty of free-market mechanisms in Lithuania provided even young inexperienced second-year students like Tomas and his friends with exceptional opportunities. For example, while at the Free Market Institute, they drafted Lithuania's commodity exchange regulations and trading rules.

This pivotal experience inspired them to start their own business. In 1990, while still second-year economics students (aged 20–22 years) they set up a limited company[12] named Libra which acted as a brokerage firm.[13] Their company's aim was to act on behalf of other firms, mainly those involved in trading activities. They were still young and not taken very seriously, especially in the beginning, but as Tomas notes, their youth and naivety were assets, since they saw this initial business as a learning experience. Their firm's services slowly gained popularity and during its brief 18 months of operation (from 1991–92) they were able to save US$50 000. This provided the start-up capital for their next business venture.

Tomas recalls that they received no support from their environment: none of their professors or lecturers even knew that they had their own business. Tomas's parents were very concerned about him going into business since they thought it would be wiser for him to spend his time studying for his university degree instead of engaging in something so unknown and risky as entrepreneurship. They were especially worried that he would go bankrupt. According to Tomas, support is very important and luckily, Tomas and his four friends could provide enough support to one another in order to sustain their commitment to their business endeavours.

Even as he continued his entrepreneurial pursuits, Tomas continued studying for his degree and received a BA degree in economics from Vilnius University. Tomas adds that he barely passed his exams, since his main attention was focused on Libra Group and not on studying for exams based on courses still utilizing the Soviet way of thinking and irrelevant to Lithuania's new free-market economy.

Development and Growth

While involved in the brokerage firm, Tomas and his friends encountered an Italian businessman who was interested in buying wood products. Tomas recalls that this seemed like a good area in which to start up a new business because they thought it would be simple. As Tomas further elaborates: 'The decision was based neither on logical conclusions nor some business strategy. We chose wood because we thought it would be simple. It did not occur to us that the sector might have great potential' (Grižibauskienė 2005).

In addition, according to Tomas, they were not scared of taking the risk of starting a new business in a completely different sector because they were young (still students at the university) and it all seemed a bit of a game.

In the beginning, they knew nothing about wood or wood-processing activities. One of their friend's fathers had a tiny carpenter's workshop in a rural town in the northeastern part of Lithuania and that's where the friends began their education in wood processing (Grižibauskienė 2005). Not surprisingly, in the beginning, they made one mistake after another but they never gave up on their business idea. As Tomas notes, 'We made a lot of mistakes; but not enough to sink us. Finally we learned the basics of the business, even though it took us about seven years' (ibid.).

Their first manufacturing company was established in 1992 and named Dominga (included within the Libra Group structure). It specialized in making wooden boards and oak furniture. By 1993, regular sales channels to Western European countries were established. After seven years of operation, in 1998 Libra Group was restructured and Libra Holding was established, which would facilitate further continuous growth of the companies held by Libra Holding. This success paved the way for the development of twelve distinct companies (shown in Table 6.3), all under the umbrella of Libra Holding. It also had a positive effect on Libra Holding's annual revenue, which has steadily increased since 1998 (Figure 6.1). A year later, in 1999, one of the original founders of Libra Group (now Libra Holding) left because, according to Tomas, he was more of an academic scientist than the rest of them. He now teaches at the university but more recently has also started up his own business, a wine club called Vyno Klubas. The other four original

Table 6.3 The 12 companies that make up Libra Holding

Year est.	Company (location)	Type of company	Main operations	Exports/characteristics
1992	Dominga (Kietaviškės)	Manufacturing	Board cutting, oak furniture	• Exports to nine countries • Biggest oak sawmill in the Baltic region
1995	Dailinta (Vievis)	Manufacturing	Glued birch panels for the furniture industry	• Exports to 15 countries • Biggest European supplier of birch glued panels in 2006
1995	Medžio Apdaila (Vilnius)	Trading	Supplying industry and consumers with wooden products for interior finishing such as wooden flooring, mouldings, cork, etc.	• Domestic sales
1996	AMG (Vievis)	Manufacturing	Birch dowels for furniture production	• Exports to 7 countries • No. 2 producer of dowels in Europe
1996	Singlis (Vilnius)	Trading	Supplying industry with tools for wood processing and also provides tool maintenance services	• Domestic sales • Average customer base: 600 companies per month
1997	Domingos Prékyba (Vilnius)	Trading	Supplying local industry with industrial equipment such as forestry machinery, kilns, forklifts, exhaust systems, etc. as well as	• Domestic sales • Average customer base: 600 companies per month

Table 6.3 (continued)

Year Est.	Company (location)	Type of company	Main operations	Exports/characteristics
			industrial accessories such as hydraulics, pneumatics, belts, etc.	
1997	Dirvonų Lentpjūvė (Rinkunai)	Manufacturing	Hardwood sawmill providing birch elements for the furniture industry	• This company secures a stable supply of raw materials to other Libra Holding companies
1999	Dominga Hardwood (Kietaviškės)	Manufacturing	Produces engineered flooring	• Exports to three countries • The first and only engineered flooring factory in the Baltics
2000	Venta[a] (Šiauliai)	Manufacturing	Furniture factory producing wooden chairs and tables	• Exports to 12 countries • No. 2 producer in Europe of wooden chairs in 2006
2002	Grandvesta (Ukmergė)	Manufacturing	Producing boxes for industrial packaging	• Domestic sales
2003	Linokompa (Elektrėnai)	Manufacturing	Producing solid wood kitchen fronts from hardwood	• Exports to five countries • Largest manufacturer of kitchen fronts in Europe
2004	Nabukas[a]	Manufacturing	Producing kitchen furniture	• Domestic sales

Note: a. Designates the two companies that were acquired by Libra Group while the remaining ten companies were all new Libra Group start-ups.

Source: Libra Group brochures and website (http://www.Libragroup.lt).

```
┌─────────────────────────────────────────────────────────┐
│                    LIBRA HOLDING                        │
└─────────────────────────────────────────────────────────┘
```

Furniture Division	**Flooring Division**	**Industry Service Division**
• Venta	• Dominga Mill	• Singlis
• Dailinta	• Dominga	• Domingos
• Linkompa	Hardwood	Prėkyba
• AMG		• Grendvesta
• Dirvonu		• Medzio Apdaila
Lentpjuve		
• Nabukas		

Source: Libra Group brochures and website (http://www.Libragroup.lt).

Figure 6.1   Libra Holding's 12 companies categorized into three divisions

founding members of Libra Group (now Libra Holding) are still actively involved in the company and hold major management positions: Tomas Juška is CEO of Libra Holding (the umbrella organization); Irmantas Rajunčius is CEO of Dominga Mill; Vilmantas Petrauskas is CEO of Domingos Prėkyba and Edvardas Tamulis is CEO of Medžio Apdaila. By 2006, the Libra Holding companies were exporting to 20 countries in 'old' Europe (Belgium, France, Germany, Italy, Netherlands, Norway, United Kingdom, Sweden, Finland, Austria, Switzerland and Denmark), 'new' Europe (Czech Republic, Slovak Republic, Poland, Estonia and Latvia), North America (USA and Canada) and Asia (Japan). In addition, Libra Holding's companies import raw materials, tools and machinery from 30 countries worldwide. As Table 6.3 further indicates, Libra Holding's twelve companies are located throughout Lithuania, many in smaller towns in rural areas.

Figure 6.1 shows a further breakdown of the three main sectors of activity that Libra Holding's companies are actively engaged in: furniture, flooring and industry service divisions.

In 1999, and then again in 2004, Libra Holding brought in additional shareholders, changing the ownership structure from 100 per cent Lithuanian to 56 per cent Lithuanian and 44 per cent foreign owned, by bringing in two Norwegian businessman. According to Tomas, having outside ownership has been very useful for Libra Holding since both foreign owners are older individuals with many years of experience. 'They act like our older brothers, providing a sounding board for new ideas and bringing in their valuable experience of Norway's mature free-market system.' This experience is especially important for Lithuanian

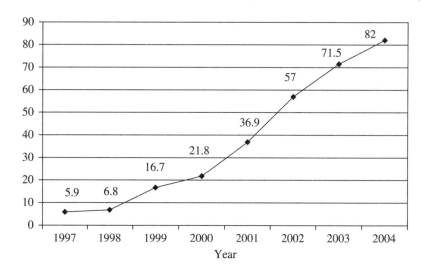

Source: Libra Holding company documents.

Figure 6.2   Libra Holding's annual revenue, 1997–2004 (€ millions)

entrepreneurs such as Tomas and his friends since their own free-market
experience has been quite brief.

In 2005, Libra Holding boasted a turnover of almost 280 million litas
(more than €81 million) which was an almost 4 per cent increase from the
previous year (270 million litas – more than €78 million). Eighteen million
litas (€5.2 million) of their 2005 turnover was reinvested. In 2006, they plan
to reach 300 million litas turnover (more than €86 million) and plan to
reinvest 15 million litas (€4.3 million).[14] In 2005, Libra Holding had 2000
employees in its twelve companies, the majority of them working in smaller
town locations in Lithuania. A summary of Libra Holding's milestones is
presented in Appendix 6.1.

Libra Holding subscribes to a very decentralized form of management
structure. Libra Holding is an umbrella organization and Tomas Juška as
its CEO is mainly involved in maintaining a 'healthy' atmosphere, supporting a high level of morale and providing a personal example which
each company's director and team can utilize to realize their own goals.
Each of the twelve companies makes its economic decisions independently.
A focus on in-company training of all employees helps reinforce the same
values among all of Libra Holding's employees.

Libra Holding's Business Philosophy

What sets Libra Holding apart from other successful businesses in Lithuania is an outspoken philosophy, which embraces far more than the bottom line. This standpoint is very much influenced by Tomas Juška. From the beginning, Tomas was focused on higher aims than simply making a profit: for example, one of Libra Holding's main business objectives is to 'create a better life in Lithuania'.

In other words, employees are motivated 'to work not just for their own good but for the good of the whole country'. In Tomas's view, Lithuanians have a deeper drive for achievement since they are trying to rebuild their native country to the level it was at before Soviet occupation fifty years ago. In that sense Lithuanians have a greater ambition to achieve excellence than their counterparts in mature market economies, or as Tomas puts it, they are 'hungrier' for success.

This humanistic philosophy seems to have paid off in terms of attracting and retaining employees. There has been virtually no turnover of upper or middle levels of management since Libra Group's establishment. Tomas is convinced that this is due to the fact that Lithuanians are much more interested in working for a company where broader values such as social responsibility and working for the greater social good are as important as making a profit.

One of Libra Holding's main strategies to maintain competitiveness is by enhancing internal human capital resources. Their business tends to be labour-intensive and since labour costs are rising in Lithuania (eroding the ability to compete in terms of cheap labour), Tomas has been focusing on training Libra Holding's staff to improve efficiency and productivity through its newly-established 'Libra School'. The concept behind 'Libra School' is to create a cultural centre which encourages, inspires and provides direction for further personal development for Libra Holding's employees.

As Tomas elaborates: 'I'm convinced that we need to improve our skills and to structure our activities in such a way as to become more competent and efficient and then we will be able to beat the competition even under civilized business rules.' He adds 'We must outdo them by being better organized, by adopting better marketing strategies and by creating a healthier work environment. Then our victory will not be short-lived' (Grižibauskienė 2005).

Tomas does not believe that his opinion or business philosophy is unique among entrepreneurs in Lithuania. The difference is that he speaks openly about the company's philosophy. While many other Lithuanian entrepreneurs may share similar values and beliefs, they are simply not accustomed to talking about them. Lithuanians are much more used to talking about their problems than about what is going well in their businesses, which Tomas feels is the 'Scandinavian approach'. However, according to Tomas, this is not necessarily the most constructive approach since it can result in people becoming overly focused on problems, which can have a demoralizing effect.

Future Plans

Though Libra Holding is the largest wood-processing company in Lithuania it is still a very small fish in the global pond and Tomas emphasizes that Libra Holding's main aim now is to maintain continual growth in terms of both product development and the countries to which they export. A recent example of product expansion is the introduction of an 'airline furniture' line in 2005.

Illustrating a mixture of social and economic aims, a long-term goal of Libra Holding is to increase its total number of employees from 2000 to 15000 individuals, which would represent approximately 1 per cent of Lithuania's total working population. Tomas highlighted that this is indeed a long-term goal and that at the moment they are in the process of reducing their employee numbers in order to increase efficiency and productivity.

As for himself, Tomas is committed to maintaining his position of CEO at Libra Holding. At 38 years of age, he feels it is the best place for him to be.

6.5   LIBRA HOLDING AND BUSINESS DEVELOPMENT DURING LITHUANIA'S TURBULENT TRANSITION: KEY FINDINGS

As Lithuania makes the transition to a market economy, entrepreneurs have experienced increasing obstacles on both the micro and macro level. The combination of increasing regulations (in the form of requirements, taxation and so on) coupled with decreasing business opportunities (due to increasing competition[15]) seem to have resulted in decreasing numbers of new private enterprises.[16] Figure 6.3 provides an indication of the frequency of changes that have taken place to tax laws in Lithuania from 1990–2000. Though a large number of businesses failed, some businesses such as Libra Holding were able to navigate comparatively easily through this changing regulatory landscape.

In Tomas's view, Lithuania's business environment was especially unstable in the early 1990s when Libra Group started its operations. But he adds that it is not such a terribly unique situation and is simply another illustration of 'doing business in a turbulent environment'. Tomas is convinced

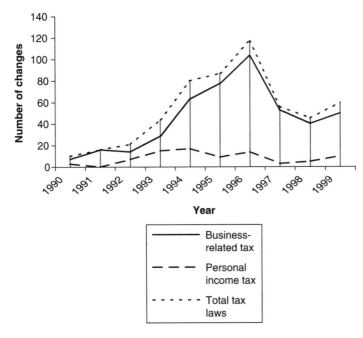

Source: Aidis (2006). Based on author's calculations from the *Lietuvos Respublikos Kodekso Rinkinys 1990–1999* (Republic of Lithuania's Regulatory Codes Index).

Figure 6.3   *The number of legislative changes to Lithuanian tax laws (new and alterations), 1999–2000*

that similar conditions occur even in advanced Western countries when a completely new business sector, such as the new technology sector, emerges. In these cases the regulatory environment is in a state of flux and businesses simply have to deal with it.

With regards to the current level of regulations and regulatory burden for Lithuanian businesses, Tomas also does not feel it is unique or unusual, since in his opinion many countries are plagued by heavy regulatory environments including old EU member countries such as Germany. As Tomas notes 'Businesses that have difficulties with regulations also have difficulties with globalization and competition.' Though Tomas adds that he would like to see more transparency of regulations in Lithuania and he feels that Lithuania is moving in this direction. New governmental initiatives such as the ability to file taxes electronically have been welcome changes for Libra Holding.

The transition process did however seem to provide rather unique business opportunities in Lithuania in the early 1990s. It would be difficult to imagine Tomas and his friends, all still students and in their early twenties, having the opportunity to start a successful business in the manufacturing sector of a non-transitional country, such as in the US, since the sector is well established and competition is fierce. But as Tomas notes, opportunities exist even in these mature markets, especially in newly emerging sectors such as IT. In addition, the case of Libra Holding illustrates the different opportunities for innovation available under vastly different economic conditions. Not only is the wood-processing sector typically not considered a sector full of opportunities, it is also a sector where little innovation could take place in established market economies. However, in Lithuania in the 1990s it was precisely the newness of the market system that provided the opportunities for innovation in wood-processing. This example again highlights the impact of the environment on the types of entrepreneurial behaviour that can be considered innovative.

In terms of opportunities during the transition process, Tomas believes that there are just as many opportunities today as there were when they started their business in 1991. But they are different in nature since the economic system was very chaotic and had no clear rules in the 1990s and today it is much more stable. Another difference has to do with the expectations of today's youth. According to Tomas, most young people today in Lithuania have unrealistic 'get rich quick' expectations. In his own case, Tomas started Libra Group with his friends when he was only 22 years of age but he was still renting a flat ten years later. 'Many young people these days expect to own their own flat at age 25.' But Tomas feels it does not work that way; 'you cannot have at 25 what you can have at 40 years of age. You need patience and hard work.'

It is also striking that Libra Holding seems to have avoided typical transition country business maladies such as a high level of corruption and regulation. For Libra Holding, the combination of a low profile and non-glamorous sector such as wood-processing and their youth and inexperience could have contributed to keeping Libra Holding off the 'radar screen' of rent-seeking officials or Mafia groups. Furthermore, Libra Holding's survival strategy seems to be simply to ignore problems in the environment.

As was typical of most private businesses start-ups in the 1990s, Libra Holding did not receive any assistance or funding from the Lithuanian government and was not able to obtain bank credits. Rather it had to depend on its own internal capabilities to survive and grow in the market.

Many researchers have noted that the lack of external financing is one of the main barriers to business development in Lithuania (Aidis 2006) as well as in other transition countries (Roman 1991; Kaganova 2002; Aidis 2003; EBRD 2002, 2005; Pissarides 2004). Usually, external financing is simply not available (Pissarides 1999; Klapper et al. 2002). Though this situation has improved in recent years through governmental initiatives in Lithuania, in the early 1990s when Tomas and his friends were just starting out, external financing was non-existent. Tomas and his friends, as with most entrepreneurs in transition countries, relied on their own savings or capital that they had acquired through a previous business to finance their business start-up and growth (see also Smallbone and Welter 2001 for further discussion). Libra Holding's case however also illustrates another characteristic of the early transitional environment, that is, the opportunities for capital accumulation. Though outside funding opportunities were lacking, opportunities to 'get rich quick' unheard of in more mature market economies were prevalent. The fact that Tomas and his friends were able to generate US$50 000 profit in their first business as a brokerage firm highlights this unique opportunity to raise large sums of money through entrepreneurial activities, even when the owners lack what would be expected in established market economies, such as experience, a track record and maturity. This reinvested capital formed the bedrock for Libra Holding's further development. Tomas also believes that the Soviet experience impacted their business choice. Though their first business was in services, Tomas and his friends were especially interested in starting a firm in manufacturing because as Tomas remarks, they were the 'children of socialism' and were more oriented towards manufacturing than services because manufacturing was always considered more important than services in the Soviet Union.

Lithuania's EU membership (in 2004) has also brought new challenges and opportunities for Libra Holding. On the one hand, Tomas complains that the EU is even more bureaucratic than the former Soviet Union, but on the other hand, Libra Holding has also been able to access EU funds to subsidize the creation of its 'Libra School'. In general, Tomas feels the two greatest benefits for Lithuania in joining the EU were firstly, the free mobility of people and secondly, the fact that it helped 'legitimize' Lithuania in the minds of many old EU countries, resulting in increased faith and less fear in doing business with Lithuania. However, since Libra Holding had already established active export ties to a number of EU countries this change did not have a great impact on its day-to-day business activities.

Tomas also believes Lithuania differs in terms of business development from most other transition countries in several distinct ways. In comparison to its Baltic neighbours (Latvia and Estonia), Tomas believes there is much more internal competition within the domestic Lithuanian market which strengthens successful local businesses and assists in their international expansion. Also the Lithuanian market has less foreign investment and as a result more domestic businesses are functioning with Lithuanian capital and management, providing greater capital returns for Lithuanian citizens. However, on a less positive note, Lithuania's complicated and unique language coupled with its lack of 'large friends' creates an isolated environment. Tomas notes that while Estonia has strong ties with Finland and Latvia has ties with Russia (due to the large percentage of Russians living in Latvia), Lithuania lacks a strong tie to any other country.

Finally, Libra Holding's case study highlights the opportunities for channelling the aspirations of transitional populations for business success. As Tomas convincingly argues, the experience of Soviet occupation increased the desire of many Lithuanians to catch up to the level of economic development enjoyed by their European neighbours. Libra Holding's aim has been to harness this patriotic drive to benefit its business activities. Their outspoken philosophy of the importance of social responsibility as well as the importance of high moral values in addition to profit making has contributed greatly to Libra Holding's success as demonstrated by its low level of employee turnover and high level of employee team spirit and morale.

6.6 CONCLUSION

Transitional environments may not seem like the most conducive situations in which to start a new business venture. In Lithuania, the early transition period was characterized by a chaotic ever-changing regulatory environment and an unstable macroeconomic environment. However the commitment to incorporating a free-market economy coupled with a historical memory of private enterprise provided a basis for new business development and growth. Indeed, the early 1990s provided tremendous business opportunities to make huge profits in previously underdeveloped sectors such as trade and other services or customer-oriented manufacturing. The Libra Holding case study illustrates this initial business development phase: it demonstrates that even relatively young and inexperienced individuals could use this newly emerging market economy to their advantage. Firstly, by starting a business in a previously non-existent sector, that is, a brokerage firm, and secondly, by using their advantageous first mover position to generate high profits. These profits were then used as start-up capital for new business development in the existing yet underdeveloped sector of wood-processing. Given the lack of outside financing for business development in Lithuania, it is unlikely that Tomas and his friends would have been able to obtain the financing necessary for manufacturing activities during early transition. Their youth and inexperience would also have severely restricted their access to outside funding in the later transition stages. However, the combination of this youth and relative naivity and a non-glamorous sector also provided advantages. It reduced interference from rent-seeking officials as well as the Mafia. While other entrepreneurs were being squeezed for bribes, Libra Group remained to a large extent off the radar screen.

Finally, though their business might not seem particularly interesting or innovative in an established market economy environment, it can be argued that in the transitional context, Libra Holding's fast-paced expansion into new domestic and international markets based on alertness to customer needs coupled with its unique business philosophy created a recipe for business success that continues into the post-transition period. The Libra Holding case illustrates that transitional turbulence can provide a fertile environment for productive entrepreneurship development.

NOTES

1. A number of individual countries recognized Lithuania's independence earlier, the first was Iceland on 29 July 1991.
2. The interim period of 'unrecognized' independence caused severe economic problems in Lithuania, largely due to the Soviet Union's economic blockade that included the refusal to supply Lithuania with fuel. In addition, repressive measures instigated by Moscow and aimed at reinforcing Soviet power in Lithuania resulted in a number of deaths, murders and hundreds of injuries.
3. Previously Soviet troops.
4. For more detailed discussion see Knobl (1993) and Saavalainen (1995).
5. Comparing the economic output in Soviet Lithuania and independent Lithuania is similar to comparing apples and oranges since the entire manner of measuring output was changed. Therefore comparing GDP levels before and after the transition process began is difficult. The exact figures may be incorrect, though we believe that the tendencies indicated are correct.
6. For example, OECD surveys of CEE countries in 1995–96 all contain a section on privatization but hardly mention new business development.
7. Since we can safely assume that the vast majority of the small enterprises (up to 19 workers) are private businesses, this table provides a good indication of the changes in growth patterns of small enterprises.
8. The number of registered SMEs is likely to include a significant percentage of inactive SMEs.
9. Lithuanian Development Agency for Small and Medium-Sized Enterprises.
10. It should be noted that Tomas studied economics as taught in the USSR which is vastly different from economics taught in free-market economies.
11. The Lithuanian Free Market Institute is a private non-profit apolitical organization established in 1990 to promote the ideas of individual freedom and responsibility, free-market philosophy and limited governmental intervention. Its driving philosophy is that the general interests of the Lithuanian people can best be realized in a free market where every individual pursues his or her objectives, without any privileges, protection or restriction (http://www.freema.org).
12. A corporation with private shareholders.
13. Underlining the complete newness of the sector, their brokerage firms code in the commodity market was 001 (Grižibauskienė 2005).
14. http://www.libragroup.lt.
15. A similar trend has been observed in Latvia (UNDP 1998).

16. We focus our study here on legally registered private enterprises, though in doing so, we are probably underestimating the true size of Lithuania's private sector. A study 'Preliminary Estimation of Monetary flows in Lithuania' carried out by the Economic Research Center of Lithuania estimates that the 'underground' or informal economy accounted for 36 per cent of GDP in 1994 and 41 per cent of GDP in 1995 (World Bank 1998). A study carried out by the Lithuanian Department of Statistics estimates that in 1995 the informal economy accounted for 23.4 per cent of GDP (Lithuanian Department of Statistics 1997). However, using the Russian case as an example, Kontorovich (1999) argues that the preferred strategy of informal activity is to register a business but hide earnings and employment. In this case, the distortion would affect the size and profitability of reported businesses more then their actual number.

REFERENCES

Acs, Z. and D. Audretsch (eds) (1993), *Small Firms and Entrepreneurship: An East-West Perspective*, Cambridge: Cambridge University Press.

Aidis, R. (2003), 'Entrepreneurship and Economic Transition', Amsterdam: Tinbergen Institute Discussion Paper, http://www.tinbergen.nl, accessed July 2006.

Aidis, R. (2006), *Laws and Customs: Entrepreneurship, Institutions and Gender During Transition*, SSEES Occasional Series, London: University College London.

European Bank for Reconstruction and Development (EBRD) (2002), *Transition Report: Agriculture and Rural Transition*, London: EBRD.

European Bank for Reconstruction and Development (EBRD) (2005), *Transition Report*, London: EBRD.

Grižibauskienė, E. (2005), 'Cottage Industries Take Off', *Lithuania in the World*, **13** (5), http://www.liw.lt.archive, accessed July 2006.

Kaganova, O. (2002), 'Small Businesses Face Large Obstacles', *Transition*, Washington, DC: The World Bank, 44–5.

Klapper, L., V. Saria-Allende and V. Sulla (2002), 'Small and Medium-Size Enterprise Financing in Eastern Europe; World Bank Policy Research Working Paper 2933, December 2002, http://www.worldbank.org, accessed July 2006.

Knobl, A. (1993), 'Lithuania', working paper, Washington, DC: International Monetary Fund (IMF).

Kontorovich, V. (1997), 'New Business Creation and Russian Economic Recovery', paper presented at the Conference on Entrepreneurship in the Transition Economies of Central and Eastern Europe, 6–7 November 1997, New York University, New York.

Kontorovich, V. (1999), 'Has New Business Creation in Russia come to a halt?', *Journal of Business Venturing*, **14**, 451–60.

Libra Holding website, http://www.libragroup.lt, accessed 5 January 2007.

Lithuanian Development Agency for Small and Medium-sized Enterprises (SMEDA) (2002), *Survey of Lithuanian SMES*, http://www.svv.lt, accessed July 2006.

Lithuanian Development Agency for Small and Medium-sized Enterprises (SMEDA) (2006), http://www.svv.lt, accessed 10 December 2006.

Lithuanian Department of Statistics (LDS) (1997), *Neapskaitoma Ekonomika: Sampratos, Tyrimai, Problemos*, Vilnius.

Pissarides, F. (1999), 'Is Lack of Funds the Main Obstacle for Growth? EBRD's Experience with Small and Medium-Sized Businesses in Central and Eastern Europe', *Journal of Business Venturing*, **14**, 520–39.

Pissarides, F. (2004), 'Financial Structures and Private Sector Development in the New Europe, in D. Masciandoro (ed.), *Financial Intermediation in the New Europe: Banks, Markets and Regulation in the Accession Countries*, Cheltenham, UK and Northampton, MA, USA: Edward Elgar, Ch. 3.

Roman, Z. (1991), 'Entrepreneurship and Small Business: The Hungarian Trajectory', *Journal of Business Venturing*, **6** (6), 447–65.

Saavalainen, T. (1995), 'Stabilization in the Baltic Countries: A Comparative Analysis', Paper, International Monetary Fund, Washington, DC.

Smallbone, D. and F. Welter (2002), 'The Distinctiveness of Entrepreneurship in Transition Economies', *Small Business Economics*, **16**, 249–62.

United National Development Program (UNDP) (1997), *Lithuanian Human Development Report*, Vilnius: UNDP.

United National Development Program (UNDP) (1998), *Latvia Human Development Report*, Riga: UNDP.

United National Development Program (UNDP) (1999), *Lithuanian Human Development Report*, Vilnius: UNDP.

World Bank (1998), *Lithuania: An Opportunity for Economic Success*, Washington, DC.

APPENDIX 6.1

Table 6A.1   Libra Holding: milestones

Year	Activity
1991	• Tomas Juška and four friends, all second-year students at Vilnius University, establish KUB Libra • Initial wood-processing begins in a small woodworking studio in the Pasvalio region of Lithuania
1992	• The start-up of Dominga, Libra Group's first wood-processing company and the beginning of the furniture division
1995	• The start-up of Dailinta and the beginning of the furniture division
1996	• The start-up of Singlis and the beginning of the industry service division
1998	• Libra Holding was established resulting in a restructuring of Libra Group's management • The first foreigner joins Libra Holding • The first strategic partnership established (with Boen from Norway)
1999	• Ragnar Ole Olsen, a Norwegian becomes the first foreign shareholder at Libra Holding
2000	• Libra Holding makes its first acquisition, the furniture factory Venta
2003	• Libra Holding establishes a strategic partnership with Nobia, the largest kitchen group in Europe • Tomas Juška, CEO of Libra Holding, is awarded the 'Laureate of the Business Hall of Fame' from Lithuania's Junior Achievement
2004	• Jens P. Heyerdahl, a Norwegian, becomes the second foreign shareholder at Libra Holding • Tomas Juška, CEO of Libra Holding, is awarded 'Manager of the Year' by the Lithuanian magazine *Veidas* • Libra School is established with the support of EU funds • Libra Holding makes its second acquisition, the furniture factory Nabukas
2005	• Libra Holding introduces a new product line: airline furniture

7. Taking advantage of transition: the case of Safety Ltd in Latvia

Arnis Sauka and Friederike Welter

INTRODUCTION

Recent studies on entrepreneurship in Latvia (for example, Kuzmina 1999), along with those conducted for other transition and new EU member countries, suggest that there are some distinctive features of entrepreneurship in a transition setting (Smallbone and Welter 2001, 2006), such as a higher level of education, a more intensive involvement in informal networks, short-term strategies and a 'learning by doing' approach. In this light, both the external environment and the distinctive personal characteristics of transition entrepreneurs can influence various types of innovation in these countries. The aim of this chapter is to provide further insight into this for a new European Union member state, namely Latvia. More specifically, we focus on revealing the influence of the specific transition context on the ability to convert new innovative opportunities into successful businesses, drawing on the case of Safety Ltd to illustrate this.

The chapter is structured as follows: the next section outlines the background for entrepreneurship and innovative businesses in Latvia, while the following two sections deal with the influence of pre start-up events on the entrepreneurial start-up decision. The fifth section concentrates on the business start-up in an early transition context, discussing issues such as developing a business idea by taking advantage of opportunities created by a specific environment. The sixth section deals with the further development of the company, before the final section offers some conclusions.

This chapter highlights the role of innovation in an external environment shaped by the previous regime and the initial transition process, including local policies and initiatives, the effects of privatization, general attitudes to entrepreneurship in society, and available human capital, as well as the importance of personal characteristics in developing innovative and successful business in Latvia. It is our view that issues influencing the development of entrepreneurship within the specific environmental setting of

Latvia, can probably best be described by persons with direct experience of them, that is the local entrepreneurs themselves. This is why we knocked on the door of one of those companies, with the intention of learning a bit more. . . .

SOME INSIGHTS INTO PRIVATE SECTOR DEVELOPMENT AND INNOVATION IN LATVIA

It is Wednesday, around 8 o'clock in the morning, but only the smell of coffee reminds us of the rather early hour. The phone rings every five minutes, people rush into the office, all with some sort of problem, most of which 'had to be solved yesterday'; and they all receive attention by the co-owner and general manager of the company 'Safety Ltd', whom we will call Peteris.[1] 'This is more or less a typical morning, not a big price to pay for a leading position in the market', Peteris says in between phone calls and frequent visits. We are in a typical Latvian company, which started its activity in the early 1990s; a period often characterized in the entrepreneurship literature as the 'early transition stage' (Smallbone and Welter 2001; Aidis and Sauka 2005). Today, the firm has more than 80 employees in Latvia, with its own manufacturing and sales departments, and it is one of the market leaders in safety equipment. What are the main determinants influencing the success of the company? This is the main question we put to Peteris. 'Well, being crazy enough even to think about starting a business in the early 1990s in Latvia, probably we were also more innovative than others in the industry.' But, considering the specific environment Latvian companies faced during the early 1990s, what kind of innovativeness are we talking about here? 'Well, that is a long story', Peteris admits. 'To understand the success of our firm and probably also innovations in Latvia at that time, we should start from the very beginning.'

The Soviet Union's leader Mikhail Gorbachev instigated reforms that resulted in the legalization of cooperatives in the late 1980s; thus, the beginnings of private sector development in Latvia are to be found under the centrally-planned system. Kuzmina (1999) refers to this period, up to the Law on Entrepreneurship in Latvia at the end of 1990, as the first stage of small business development. 'As far as I remember', says Peteris, 'most of these cooperatives were supported by the state. Buying products or raw materials for very low prices, so-called *state prices*, and selling at market price level ensured a very high level of profit. At that time 1000 per cent profit would not be anything uncommon.'

In 1991 Latvia declared its independence from the Soviet Union and transition started, with legal and market reforms, including the liberalization of purchase prices, which resulted in the cooperatives losing their advantageous position in the market. Privatization was another way to start a business at that time. These, as well as other reforms initiated the mushrooming of small and medium-sized enterprises (SMEs) in Latvia and can be classified as the second transition stage of entrepreneurship development (Kuzmina 1999). This was followed by the 'contemporary stage of entrepreneurship development' from 1994 onwards, the third stage of entrepreneurial development in Latvia (ibid.). As a result of this development, Latvia, with a population of 2.4 million inhabitants, approximately one-third of whom live in the capital city Riga, had approximately 54 000 legally registered SMEs in 2005, which constitutes an increase of about 10 000 since 2000 (CSB 2006a). Further, since 1994, there has been a positive tendency in most other economic indicators. By the end of 2005 Latvia's GDP per capita reached US$11 962, with an almost constant growth in real GDP since 1995, and the increase in the private sector share in GDP, growing from 55 per cent in 1994 to 70 per cent in 2005 (EBRD 2003, 2005). However, as illustrated by Table 7.1, both in terms of the business environment and economic development, Latvia still lags behind most of the other new EU countries.

Regarding innovation in SMEs in a transition context, only a few studies have analysed this issue for the early stages of transition (for example, Smallbone et al. 2000). This is no surprise in Latvia, as the earliest initiatives from policymakers aimed at promoting the innovativeness of SMEs only started in the mid-1990s. Today, however, a knowledge-based economy founded on competitive and innovative companies is highlighted as a major priority. Further, surveys on the innovativeness of Latvian companies, conducted after 2000, reflect positive tendencies with regard to the introduction of various innovations (CSB 2006b). For instance, almost 20 per cent of the total number of firms registered in Latvia were considered as innovative[2] in the period from 2001 to 2004 (CSB 2006b). Surveys, however, conclude that most innovations in Latvia are implemented by big companies; which again raises the question about how innovation is defined and measured.

Regardless of this, recent studies place Latvian SMEs among the least innovative in the European Union (Lopez-Claros et al. 2005; Dombrovsky et al. 2005; European Commission 2005). However, these studies do not address the issue of different types of innovation that may be present in the early stages of transition. That is, whether the specific transition environment influenced the type of innovation and how at least some of today's successful companies took advantage of the specific context characterizing this period. To answer these questions, we return to Peteris, the co-owner of Safety Ltd.

Table 7.1 Business environment and economic development in new EU countries

	Bulgaria	Czech R.	Estonia	Hungary	Latvia	Lithuania	Poland	Romania	Slovak R.	Slovenia	OECD
GDP (in billion US$ 2004)[a]	24.1	107	11.2	100.3	13.5	22.3	241.8	73.2	41.1	32.2	
Private sector share in GDP in 2005[a] (%)	70	80	80	80	70	75	75	70	80	65	
Inflation 2005 estimation[a] (%)	4.2	2	3.9	3.8	6.4	2.8	2.2	9.2	2.4	2.5	
Unemployment rate[b] (%)	13.6	7.8	10.1	5.8	10.5	12.7	19.2	6.6	17.1	6.5	
Starting a business (per cap income)[c]	7.9	8.9	5.1	20.9	3.5	2.8	21.4	4.4	4.8	9.4	5.3
Hiring workers (% salary)[c]	30.1	35	33.5	35.2	24.1	31.2	21.4	33	35.2	16.6	21.4
Firing costs (weeks of wages)[c]	8.7	21.7	34.7	34.5	17.3	30.3	13	3	13	39.6	31.3
Registering property (% property value)[c]	2.3	3	0.7	11	2	0.7	2	1.9	0.1	2	4.3

| Enforcing a contract (% debt)[c] | 14 | 14.1 | 11.5 | 9.6 | 11.8 | 8.6 | 10 | 10.7 | 15.7 | 15.2 | 11.2 |
| Closing a business (% estate)[c] | 9 | 14.5 | 9 | 14.5 | 13 | 7 | 22 | 9 | 18 | 8 | 7.1 |

Sources: a. EBRD (2005); b. UNECE (2003), www.unece.org; c. World Bank Doing Business Indicators, www.doingbusiness.org.

CHOOSING ENTREPRENEURSHIP: EVIDENCE FROM THE EARLY TRANSITION STAGE

'Vacuum is the best word to describe the situation in the Latvian market during the early 1990s', Peteris continues, referring to the lack of various goods and services that people take for granted today, which opened up good business opportunities. Even more importantly, the supply market was far from being developed, as Peteris ironically remembers: 'People were just getting used to the market economy, and they did not really know what they wanted.' This was the situation at the time when Peteris started his first business back in 1992, a small wood-working company, a choice which reflected Latvia's natural resources.

Finding and realizing new profit opportunities is often mentioned as one of the main challenges during the early transition setting (Webster 1993). Lack of previous entrepreneurship experience, a characteristic specific to the early transition entrepreneur (Kusnezova 1999), makes this even more complicated. Peteris was among those who obtained capital through the privatization process. Unfortunately (or perhaps fortunately), in less than a year his first company went bankrupt. Even today, however, Peteris thinks that his first business had good potential for development. 'Something did not work out, but I can always blame the situation in the market', he jokes, possibly not without reason, considering the situation of Latvia's emerging market system in the early 1990s. 'I will not talk about entrepreneurship-related legislation and similar constraints here, as these were only starting to develop at that time. Latvia was like a child, only two or three years old, and you cannot expect a lot from anyone at that age, can you? It was more difficult from the psychological point of view.' Indeed, apart from macro-economic stability, inflation, and business regulation, one of the biggest challenges for entrepreneurs during early transition was the attitude of government and society (Smallbone and Welter 2001). 'Wherever I went, I was considered a criminal . . . "entrepreneur" and "criminal" were almost synonyms at that time in Latvia and trust me, that is a very big pressure, especially in the start-up phase of a firm', Peteris recalls.

'On the other hand, I was probably too young and inexperienced and would not have succeeded in a more stable environment. And from this perspective it was a good lesson.' Well, obviously not only for him, as 'learning by doing' was a common approach to gaining business experience in transition countries (Aidis 2006). Be that as it may, Peteris was without a job and money, open to anything to make his life 'human'. 'How did I proceed? Well, actually it was three of us, all only 23 years old, who proceeded . . . There were three friends from high school . . .', perhaps this is how we should have started this story. Even at school they were thinking about 'doing something to get rich'. As Peteris perceives it, the easiest way to do that was using 'old networks'. Indeed, in the early stages of transition, so-called informal networks were often used to mobilize resources and obtain orders, to help with coping with bureaucracy and dealing with unfriendly officials (for example, Smallbone and Welter 2001). But Peteris and his friends were too young to have such networks and they did not want to become involved in criminal activities, which, according to Peteris, was not uncommon as a way of earning money at that time: 'Actually, I am quite sure that the majority of entrepreneurs, some of them very successful and well-known in society today, raised their capital in one of these ways.' Having had his own business, he was the first of the three to start on the way to achieving this as yet only vaguely defined aim of 'getting rich'. But the other two were also involved in business activities, which, seen from today's perspective, helped to shape the current business orientation of the company.

One of the friends, Juris, who is the second co-owner of the company, was in a rather 'slippery' business at that time. He worked for one of those companies involved in so-called 'pyramid schemes'. Anyone living in Latvia or other transition countries in the early 1990s will remember these schemes. They allowed you to buy a certificate for a certain sum and the obligation to sell a certain number of certificates to others. In turn, those people sold certificates to others and so on, creating the pyramid. This was not exactly a legal activity at that time; moreover, a number of pyramid companies, including the one Juris was involved in, were simply cheating their customers, earning quick money and disappearing. This reflects both the 'short-term' and 'get-rich-quick' strategies and involvement in the official and informal economies, characteristics often highlighted as being specific to entrepreneurship during transition, especially in the early stages of market reform (Roberts and Tholen 1998; Kontorovich 1999; Smallbone and Welter 2006). 'The experience that Juris got while working for that company was not without a lesson', says Peteris. The biggest benefit was that they understood that it is also possible to start a business completely from scratch, 'getting money from nowhere', although this 'should not be done illegally, of course'. However, considering that business legislation was very much in the early stages of development, what was legal and what was illegal? 'Indeed, there were many gaps in the legislation at that time', agrees Peteris, 'and often it was only conscience and common sense that kept you away from getting involved in activities that were clearly illegal, yet not forbidden by law.'

So, Peteris and Juris were almost in the same position, both without a job and money. But, there was also the third friend, Ivars, who today is no longer involved in the business. 'He did not have any business experience, he was simply a tailor without a job', Peteris remembers with a smile. More specifically, he had lost a job in one of the big factories that collapsed along with the Soviet Union. He was nevertheless engaged in 'informal business', namely sewing clothes for individual customers. 'At the time we suggested making this "hobby" into a real business; actually, things were going pretty well for him. It was the aim "to get rich" that we all shared that made it so easy to persuade him, I guess', says Peteris. 'Three people, different backgrounds, but the same dream, this is how we started.'

DEVELOPING A BUSINESS IDEA IN THE TRANSITION SETTING

Uncertainty is often mentioned as one of the most important features of the environment in which entrepreneurship in transition countries functions (Van de Mortel 2002). A cause for this uncertainty often highlighted in the literature is the total collapse of the social, political, and economic order, which characterized transition countries in the late 1980s and early 1990s. In the context of transition, all the problems of uncertainty facing Western firms exist. In addition, however, entrepreneurs face a wide range of new sources of unpredictable factors that can potentially affect their activities (EBRD 1995). This is something that our conversation with Peteris also reflects: 'Considering the nature of the environment I had already experienced with my first business, we had no idea how this would all look like and whether it would be possible at all. All or nothing, these are probably the words best describing the situation of this start-up back in 1994.'

With one of them having expertise in sewing clothes, the three decided to start manufacturing men's suits. They had some previous business experience, a couple of sewing machines and also some money borrowed from friends to buy fabric. 'Initially, our main advantage at that time was the market gap', Peteris remembers. 'There was a potential demand for so many things in the market that even the blind would have noticed it!' Big shopping chains offering men's suits, such as Dressman for instance, had not yet entered the market and Peteris and his friends decided to try to fill this gap. It should be noted that apart from Ivar's knowledge as a tailor, no further market research was done prior to starting the business. 'We simply could not afford it – with what resources?' asks Peteris rhetorically.

The innovativeness of the start-up did not consist of introducing a new product or service, as Peteris explains: 'Amongst other things, it was rather an attitude, maybe not so easily understandable from today's perspective. From the first day of our business activity we were concentrating on quality and service for both our products and our newly-established brand.' This sounds very obvious today, does it not? But at that time, if you could buy anything in Latvia, it was typically a cheap and poor quality product. According to Peteris, in an immature market such as the Latvian one at that time a demand for quality still had to be created.

When the first suits were ready for sale, the immature nature of the market showed itself in a manner not very encouraging for the company: good quality suits appeared to be far too expensive. 'Obviously the market was not yet ready for this type of supply', reflects Peteris. Two choices were open to them: either educate the market themselves and enjoy the benefits from being the first, or change their strategy by offering suits of a lower, but still good, quality. A lack of resources determined the second choice – the company changed its strategy to meet the market demand. But just when the first suits were being sold, some of the big clothing chains entered the market . . . 'It was some kind of "shock"', remembers Peteris. 'We anticipated this, of course, but nobody expected that it would happen so fast. We felt – and actually were – too small to compete with them, considering the resources we had.' They were still trying to work in this direction, as a number of ready-made suits were already in stock together with some fabric. It was clear, however, that the company would not be able to compete in this market.

'When searching for the fabric for suits, we sent lots of letters to possible suppliers across Europe, including Germany', recalls Peteris. What happened next was not planned, but nonetheless actually shaped the business orientation of the company towards what it is today. One of his friends was buying a car in Germany. It was quite common in those times: many people did it as it offered the opportunity of buying a relatively good car cheaply. 'As I knew some German, he asked me to go to Germany to pick up the car, which I did', remembers Peteris. While in Germany, he visited a couple of manufacturers and distributors of fabric, companies they had contact with. In one of these he picked up a catalogue of uniforms for shop assistants. 'This caught my attention as it was something completely new for me and as it turned out later, also for the Latvian market. If you had seen the shop assistants' uniforms in Latvia at that time!' he remembers, trying to find some old leaflets.

Back in Latvia they prepared offers and sent them to shop managers across the country, still without too many expectations. 'Who might have thought that people would buy something like this here?' exclaims Peteris. 'And who might have thought that you can make business out of uniforms for shop assistants? Why not, one might ask? Well, simply because it was something completely new for the Latvian market, call it innovation, call it what you will. It was simply not a common way of thinking, for example, that you should spend money to make shops look good, or that builders should wear appropriate and good quality safety work-wear, for example.' So they were not really surprised that nobody answered their offer letters. 'After a second week of silence we already decided to think about some other ways to start our business', remembers Peteris. 'But then, all of a sudden, the doors of our tiny office opened and a guy came in holding the pictures in his hand asking "where the hell can I get all these things you offer?" ' This is how they started in the uniform and safety equipment business back in 1994.

'Things like this would not be possible these days, at least not so easily. The market is overwhelmed with various types of goods and you can not simply go abroad and pick up something you have not seen in Latvia and try to sell it here. It is much more complicated today', declares Peteris. Still, and at least at the early stage of transition, these actions can be seen as a type of 'innovativeness', with firms using underdeveloped markets to 'transfer' products, both physical goods and knowledge, with the aim of creating profits. This aspect still has not received proper attention in the transition literature.

DEVELOPMENT THROUGH INNOVATION: TAKING ADVANTAGE OF THE TRANSITION CONTEXT

Thus, the company moved into a completely new area. Contacts with other possible suppliers of work-wear and safety equipment were soon established, while more and more firms in Latvia were willing to buy these products. 'True, we had a successful business idea, but there are other reasons why we succeeded in developing it into a successful business', emphasizes Peteris. First of all they were willing to grow, which is not typical for small businesses in general (Wiklund et al. 2003). To be more specific: 'Our success, as well as the main challenges, during the company's initial period of development was shaped by the following features: good quality goods new to the market, sales strategy, and control of resources.' As a result, the company was able to achieve continuous growth, about 20 per cent a year, reaching 85 employees and a turnover of €3 million by the end of 2005. So let us take a closer look at the determinants influencing the successful development of the company.

'Looking back, we were innovative by being first', says Peteris. By 'being first', however, he does not mean offering new products or services as such. These were already developed and sold across the world. What the company did was to bring these products to a new market. So although there were already firms selling safety equipment on the market, most of them could not be considered competitors as they were offering cheap, poor quality 'Soviet standard' goods. 'We were different: focusing on quality, so-called "Western standards", and have remained as such until now', says Peteris. It sounds easy, does it not? 'Well, it was not exactly so, and very often still is not even now in 2006.'

Offering products that were different was one of the determinants of the company's success story and also the biggest challenge. 'The problem at the beginning was that people simply were not used to spending money for good quality, regardless of whether you were offering a suit or a safety boot. Advertisement slogans such as "this safety boot is specially designed for builders and will protect their feet from possible accidents at work" or "to ensure your employees' safety we suggest using specially designed gloves for welding" were often not considered. People were used to "buying price" not quality even if it was a matter of safety; and we were one of the first companies that changed this situation in Latvia, at least in our field.'

'Bringing products to the market is not enough – you still need to sell them', says Peteris – half jokingly, half seriously. Indeed, the *sales strategy* is another determinant of the company's success and in this particular case also a type of innovation more 'relevant' to the transition setting. 'Our sales strategy from the very beginning was based on one of the "truths of the world": people choose what is most convenient for them and are reluctant to give it up easily for something else', explains Peteris. What they did was, again, nothing new at all: they used a direct sales strategy. Various firms, such as those selling cosmetics, started applying direct sales almost from the very beginning of private sector development in Latvia. For the distribution of safety equipment, however, this was something unprecedented. In practice, all sales managers have their own customers that they are responsible for, right from the first contact until after-sales service. Sales managers constantly look after the customer, offering new products, and they are motivated because their salaries depend on the sales volume. In this way, they created a network of customers with the advantage of direct contact, which allowed for getting to know the customers' needs.

Direct sales, or more exactly 'direct motivation' of sales managers to look after their customers, ensured another 'innovative action' within the industry: *after-sales service*. 'If one sells a poor quality, cheap product, this is not really an issue. Our strategy was to focus on good quality and thus more expensive products brought this "obligation" up', explains Peteris. Overall, however, the direct sales approach requires high-level expertise from sales personnel in terms of knowing the product. 'At the beginning it was easy, as we did not have such a variety as today on offer', Peteris recalls, 'But using both self-motivation mechanisms as well as various seminars on new and existing products organized within the company we manage this process pretty well.'

And finally, *control of resources* was another important determinant of the company's success and one which is often neglected by small firms in their early stages of development. 'Lack of control over internal processes within the company was the main reason for the bankruptcy of my first business and a lot of start-ups in Latvia during the early 1990s', says Peteris, emphasizing the role of various control mechanisms, at that time in Latvia used only by some big companies. 'But you do not make the same mistake twice!' He further describes how in the first months of their business they designed computer software that still helps to look after all kinds of processes within the company. These include lists of existing and potential customers for each manager, products sold by each manager and turnover and profits generated, debtors, general product flow on stock, cash flow, and so on. 'With this software we always know what is happening in the company, which products we need to order, which manager should be motivated, and so on. Knowing exactly where you are allows you to develop a feasible strategy and plan investments', says Peteris. 'This is always an important issue, but it was really crucial in the very early stages of our business.'

These are the main determinants of start-up success, but what about problems and challenges during the development phase of the company? According to Peteris, there were several. However, almost all new companies regardless of the business environment face such problems. The only challenge to highlight here is actually closely linked with one of the success determinants of Safety Ltd, namely its direct sales. The 'problem' here was that some sales managers worked so well that they won many big customers; and subsequently, some of them decided they could manage without the company and so they left and started their own business. 'We have had several such cases in the past, actually in this way we have "created" two companies, who are our competitors today', says Peteris. 'Well, life is life and I wish them luck, of course. But I also do not think that something like this would be possible in our firm today, as we have created several mechanisms, for instance not allowing one manager to work with big customers on their own, to avoid such situations.'

MOVING FORWARD: REFLECTING ON YESTERDAY, TODAY, AND INSIGHTS INTO THE FUTURE

'We have always been oriented to long-term business. And this was not common, especially for the early 1990s in Latvia', says Peteris, confirming empirical evidence from various studies on entrepreneurship in transition (for example, Smallbone and Welter 2001). No doubt many businesses in

Latvia today are long-term oriented. But anecdotal evidence also tells many stories about 'new companies' set up in the early 1990s to earn quick profits but which quickly disappeared. 'After some time you see the same people managing a company with another name and maybe also in another industry', says Peteris. 'And – trust me – these are very "innovative" people in ways of "doing business". Not paying for large amounts of goods after gaining the trust of suppliers is but one example of these "innovations".'

What is unique for transition countries, however, is that companies can develop alongside the development of the environment as a whole. And this is what has happened to Safety Ltd. 'If you want to move forward, both business development as well as changes in the general environment require certain actions', emphasizes Peteris. Some of these, determining the most recent developments of the firm, are highlighted in this section, together with some insight into the future plans of the company.

The role of sales strategy as a determinant of success during the early development phase has already been mentioned, but we have not talked about suppliers. In an advanced transition environment such as Latvia, this is yet another dimension where the company shows some 'innovativeness'. Following a long-term business orientation meant establishing reliable supply chains and continually working to maintain them as one of the main priorities of the firm during the last four or five years. According to Peteris, this is important for three reasons: first, product development; second, product quality; and third, setting the best prices for the best quality. 'These were suppliers who in recent years helped us to develop our product assortment as it is now. We always listen to the advice of our suppliers, even now, having a lot more expertise in our field of business. And, of course, our suppliers care about the quality of the goods they deliver – after all, we are a good, long-term customer for them.'

Buying in large quantities and working together with its suppliers over an extended period of time also provides advantages for Safety Ltd, such as fewer or reduced advance payments, faster deliveries and better prices. All this taken together has helped the company to grow. However, it is also the case that once the sales volume grows, companies such as Safety Ltd can afford even 'better suppliers'. 'Probably we were one of the first companies in Latvia who started to work directly with manufacturers from China in our field of business', says Peteris. 'Currently we are buying lots of good quality goods from there and this is the best price for the best quality goods in our market.' Initially, they had to survive their customers' mistrust of the 'made in China' brand, as it was considered to be cheap and poor quality, 'something quite the opposite to what customers were expecting from us'.

'Today we are in a complex business, but this is something every firm should consider if it wants to go for development', says Peteris. He also emphasizes that no longer are Latvian companies working in an immature, underdeveloped market, regardless of the fact that private sector development in Latvia started only some 15 years ago. 'Those days are gone in Latvia. Today we face fierce competition both locally and from international companies. Working in such an environment requires even more emphasis on product and service quality, and this is one of our major strategies today.' Safety Ltd is one of the first in the industry in Latvia that is adjusting products to meet all EU safety standards: 'At some point it is necessary to do a lot of paper work, and so on, to get everything ready according to these requirements; and this took almost half a year and considerable financial resources.' Peteris emphasizes, however, that they are among the first in Latvia to operate with all necessary certification and other documentation for each safety item. He is even more satisfied that these investments are already starting to generate returns. Increasingly, companies are choosing to follow safety requirements although in Latvia these have already been laid down by law since the late 1990s. According to North (1990), such behaviour reflects the often-conflicting role between formal rules – such as established laws and regulations – and informal rules, such as the attitudes of people towards new rules, specific for the transition environment, which obviously also applies in the more advanced stages of development in Latvia.

How about other strategies for the future development of the business? 'Well, we do not plan too much expansion in the Latvian market as it is not made of rubber', Peteris grins. 'But why not try some other market?' he adds. The company has recently established a business in Ukraine and this is going fairly well. With its headquarters located in Kiev and seven small branches scattered throughout Ukraine, they now provide coverage to the whole country. Apart from this, they also have a couple of other businesses, mostly dealing with real estate. 'As time goes by, some companies are being established having nothing to do with our work-wear and safety equipment. Some of these are successful, some not, but this is probably already another story, I guess', he adds.

'How do I feel about all this myself?' muses Peteris, still only 37 years old, when asked about his own plans for the future. 'Well, to tell the truth, not too excited . . . but maybe this is because of autumn. There are probably still some challenges left for me in this type of business, especially in Ukraine, but should I take them? Maybe it is worth selling the company in Latvia and thinking about something else in my life? What makes it even more difficult and has always been my concern is that it is very difficult, even impossible, to do fair business in Latvia – informal networks, corruption both in private and public sectors, various types of cheating as well as late payments are still not uncommon. Some would argue that the situation has changed over the past 10 years. Still, "under the surface" a lot of things, including corruption on the various levels, have remained the same. We have only learned to both label and approach these things differently. Instead of corruption we talk about lobbying, and the methods to gain orders have also changed, e.g. only few people still pay in cash for the "favour". Strategies far more complicated than these have been developed but I prefer not to talk about these issues in detail. Anyway, this is something I could never get used to even over all these years . . . Well, this is today', he says sitting comfortably in his chair, 'but tomorrow is tomorrow. Let's see what we come up with then . . .', leaving us with the impression, though, that we will hear some new success stories about this firm as it develops further.

SOME FINAL CONCLUSIONS

The entrepreneurship literature argues that it is not appropriate to analyse entrepreneurial activity without considering the context in which compa-nies work (Karlsson and Dahlberg 2003). By shaping the role and actions of entrepreneurs, the context is of special importance in countries under-going changes while moving from one regime to another, as is the case with transition countries. Considering the specific environment facing entrepre-neurs in various transition countries, as well as different stages of transi-tion development within each particular country, the question arises how this influences the nature of entrepreneurship in these countries.

Empirical studies have identified a number of barriers facing SMEs at different stages of transition (Aidis and Sauka 2005), such as lack of pre-vious entrepreneurship traditions, an imperfect legislative framework and the negative attitudes of government and society towards entrepreneurship. Far less attention, however, has been paid to the opportunities offered by the transition environment. By using the case of a Latvian company, this study partly fills the gap. The case of Safety Ltd and its co-owner Peteris illustrates how the environment can contribute to opportunities during transition, but also shows that entrepreneurial alertness is required to iden-tify and exploit such opportunities, thus confirming that opportunities are not only out there, but they are also created by entrepreneurs.

More specifically, the case demonstrates how entrepreneurs can gain advantage from transition conditions by focusing on distinctive types of innovativeness. The methodology used to address this question does not allow generalizing the findings, nor is this the intention. Whilst suggesting the necessity for further research on the topic, the case sheds some light on specific types of innovation during various stages of transition as well as various phases of company development. Being first in the business is often not the best for one simple reason. Your competitors can simply copy your 'innovations' and often make money by using your investment. This notion, however, refers to activities which can be copied easily, for example, new product design. Findings from the case study suggest that the situation is different if we consider the strategies and orientation of a given business. Obviously, the orientation of Peteris and his colleagues on innovations is one of the decisive determinants influencing the company's success during various stages of transition.

But what is so 'innovative' about the strategies used by this particular firm? Safety Ltd is a fairly typical company, using strategies one could find in almost any textbook today. We would argue that innovativeness here consists in these activities being implemented in a specific environment, characterized by a lack of knowledge about such strategies; the same also applies to the products sold, as in the case of this particular case study. 'We did not re-invent the bicycle', says Peteris, 'we were only able to transfer knowledge from the West, adjusting to the situation in our market. And we did it first. Call it innovation or use some other word for it, but this helped us to achieve the leading position in the market.' Indeed, we cannot really consider the strategies initiated by this firm as any different from those introduced by companies in more advanced market economies. But what becomes obvious from the case is the role entrepreneurial alertness has to play in a transition environment, thus emphasizing the importance of human capital in developing innovative businesses. In this context, Peteris and his colleagues have to be given credit for their initiative. Initiative in being the first to do something that others either dare not do or simply have not done because of a lack of knowledge, while the entrepreneurs in this case never let the lack of knowledge hamper their business ideas.

ACKNOWLEDGEMENTS

Financial support from the TeliaSonera Institute at the Stockholm School of Economics in Riga is gratefully acknowledged.

NOTES

1. All names and the company name are pseudonyms.
2. Innovation here is defined as 'new or significantly improved product (commodity or service) introduced onto the market or the introduction of a new or significantly improved process within an enterprise. The innovation should be new to the enterprise, but it need not necessarily be new to the market.'

REFERENCES

Aidis, R. (2006), *By Laws and Customs: Entrepreneurship, Institutions and Gender During Transition*, SSEES Occasional Series, University College London, London.

Aidis, R. and A. Sauka (2005), 'Entrepreneurship in a Changing Environment: Analyzing the Impact of Transition Stages on SME Development', in F. Welter (ed.), *Challenges in Entrepreneurship and SME Research*, InterRENT 2005 online publication, www.ecsb.org.

Central Statistical Bureau of Latvia (2006a), *Statistical Bulletin*, Riga, Latvia.

Central Statistical Bureau of Latvia (2006b), *Research and Development Innovation Statistics*, Statistical Data Collection, Riga, Latvia.

Dombrovsky, V., M. Chandler and K. Kreslins (2005), *Global Entrepreneurship Monitor 2005 Latvia Report*, TeliaSonera Institute, Riga, Latvia.

European Bank for Reconstruction and Development (1995), *Transition Report 1995*, London: EBRD.

European Bank for Reconstruction and Development (2003), *Transition Report 2003*, London: EBRD.

European Bank for Reconstruction and Development (2005), *Transition Report 2005*, London: EBRD.

European Commission (2005), *European Innovation Scoreboard 2005. Comparative Analysis of Innovation Performance*, Luxembourg: European Commission.

Karlsson, C. and R. Dahlberg (2003), 'Entrepreneurship, Firm Growth and Regional Development in the New Economic Geography: Introduction', *Small Business Economics*, **21**, 73–6.

Kontorovich, V. (1999), 'Has New Business Creation in Russia Come to a Halt?' *Journal of Business Venturing*, **14** (5/6), 451–60.

Kusnezova, N. (1999), 'Roots and Philosophy of Russian Entrepreneurship', *Journal for East European Management Studies*, **4** (1), 45–72.

Kuzmina, I. (1999), 'Economic and Social Aspects of Entrepreneurship in Latvia during Transition to the Market Economy', PhD thesis (in Latvian), University of Latvia, Riga, Latvia.

Lopez-Claros, A., E. Porter and K. Schwab (2005), *Global Competitiveness Report 2005–2006. Policies Underpinning Rising Prosperity*, Basingstoke: Palgrave Macmillan.

North, D. (1990), *Institutions, Institutional Change, and Economic Performance*, Cambridge: Cambridge University Press.

Roberts, K. and J. Tholen (1998), 'Young Entrepreneurs in East-Central Europe and the Former Soviet Union', *IDS Bulletin*, **29**, 59–64.

Smallbone, D., N. Isakova, A. Slonimski, E. Aculai and F. Welter (2000), 'Small Business in the Ukraine, Belarus and Moldova: Employment, Innovation, Regional Development', *Belarussian Economic Journal*, **3**, 40–49 (in Russian).

Smallbone, D. and F. Welter (2001), 'The Distinctiveness of Entrepreneurship in Transition Economies', *Small Business Economics*, **16**, 249–62.

Smallbone, D. and F. Welter (2006), 'Conceptualising Entrepreneurship in a Transition Context', *International Journal of Entrepreneurship and Small Business*, **3** (2), 190–206.

Van de Mortel, E. (2002), *An Institutional Approach to Transition Processes*, Aldershot, UK: Ashgate.

Webster, L.M. (1993), 'The Emergence of the Private Sector Manufacturing in Poland. A Survey of Firms', World Bank Technical Paper, no. 237, Washington, DC: World Bank.

Wiklund, J., P. Davidsson and F. Delmar (2003), 'What Do They Think and Feel About Growth? An Expectancy-Value Approach to Small Business Manager's Attitudes Toward Growth', *Entrepreneurship, Theory and Practice*, Spring, 247–70.

8. Being entrepreneurial in Poland: new conditions, new opportunities, new undertakings

Anna Rogut and Kazimierz Kubiak

INTRODUCTION

Polish entrepreneurship has long traditions, reaching back to the nine-teenth century. It continued to develop even during the decades of the centrally-planned economy, entering a true renaissance period in the 1980s, when it was used as a vehicle for limited reforms of Poland's socialist economy (Piasecki 1997). The 1990s brought even more incentives for the further development of entrepreneurship, with the launching of the process of political and economic transition. In particular, it was the latter phenomenon that greatly contributed to transforming the 'entrepreneurial spirit' in thousands of Polish people into an active force committed to the development of a variety of forms of private business. As a result, the 1990s saw a more than fivefold increase in the number of registered private businesses (mostly small and medium-sized), reaching 2 915 821 at the end of 1999 (Dzierżanowski and Stachowiak 2001).

This phenomenon was accompanied by a gradual change in the perception of the role of the entrepreneur (Rogut 2002). Whereas in the first stage of the transformation it followed the Schumpeterian tradition where 'new firms with the entrepreneurial spirit displace less innovative incumbents, ultimately leading to a higher degree of economic growth' (Audretsch 2003, p. 5), later on, the Kirzner tradition prevailed, which stressed the ability to observe the market and the readiness to take advantage of opportunities unnoticed by others (Kirzner 1979).

A good example of the latter tradition is Mieczysław Kozera, who is the main protagonist of this chapter. He is 'able to "see" opportunities, and take advantage of those opportunities across national markets, if not the world as a whole, wherever there are discrepancies (or market failures)' (Etemad 2004, p. 15).

GREEN LIGHT FOR THE DEVELOPMENT OF
ENTREPRENEURSHIP

Poland, with its population of over 38 million people and area of nearly 314 000 square kilometres, is by far the largest new member state of the European Union. It is a country that entered the twenty-first century with a rapidly growing economy. However, its economy has not been developing fast enough to close the gap separating it from the vast majority of national economies in the EU. In 2006, with its GDP per capita amounting to nearly US$12 900 (EBRD 2006), Poland occupied one of the very last positions (Council of Ministers 2005).

The inflow of foreign capital, which is in the range of 2 to 6 per cent of GDP annually, plays an important role in the Polish economy. For instance, in 2005 the inflow of foreign capital reached US$8.7 billion, thus placing Poland in second place among the new member states of the European Union. Foreign investments are an important source of transfer of innovations to the Polish industry. However, they do not replace domestic investments, but are rather complementary (Polish Information and Foreign Investment Agency 2006).

In the 1990s, the ownership structure in the Polish economy underwent a substantial reconstruction, and the role of the private sector in the national economy strongly intensified. The catalysts for these changes were a rapid development of the small and medium-size enterprise sector (SME) and privatization of state companies. At the end of 2005, there were 3 579 800 firms operating in Poland,[1] and 96 per cent of them were private ventures (Central Statistical Office 2006b).

A dynamic development of the private sector has placed Poland in the group of countries with a high level of entrepreneurship, measured by the total entrepreneurial activity (TEA) index.[2] In 2004, it reached 8.83 per cent, against an average of 9.41 per cent for all 34 countries participating in the Global Entrepreneurship Monitor (GEM) at that time. As a result, Poland was classified twelfth out of all 34, and first among European countries (Bacławski et al. 2005). However, a deeper qualitative analysis of entrepreneurship (including motivation, introducing innovations, focus on fast growth, social potential and so on) reveals that Poland is not a more entrepreneurial country than, for example, Belgium or the Netherlands, which scored lower on the TEA index. Although Poland has a quantitative advantage, it lags behind in terms of creating the right environment for the development of entrepreneurship (financial support, education, commercial support, physical infrastructure and so on).

A prominent place in that environment is occupied by administrative barriers that are the result of legal regulations imposed by national legislation. These barriers significantly increase the difficulty of, among other things, registering companies, getting licences/permits, and purchasing/leasing land. Although a certain set of administrative procedures seems indispensable for defining the relationship between economy and public administration institutions, an excess of administrative procedures is a burden on the economy, limiting its potential. And this is exactly what is happening in Poland.

Despite the fact that since the beginning of the transformation numerous attempts have been made to limit the bureaucratic burden on the economy, the great number of complicated, time-consuming procedures remains an obstacle. For instance, according to the World Bank, the number of procedures required for starting a business in Poland was approximately ten in 2005, higher than that in other OECD countries (except for the Czech Republic and Slovenia), where the average number of procedures does not exceed six (World Bank 2005).

Other problematic issues are the complexities and changeability of laws regulating many administrative procedures, especially investment processes (building and reconstruction permits, permits of usage), and tax law. In the former case, most difficulties arise from inconsistent regulations and the overlapping of competences of various institutions (Polish Information and Foreign Investment Agency 2003; Ministry of Economy and Labour Affairs 2004). On the other hand, the 'black list' of tax law defects includes excessive legislation (several different types of income tax, a great number of exceptions, exemptions, deductions and so on), substantial variability of regulations, which significantly increases economic risk, and lack of uniform legal interpretations (discrepant interpretations issued by different authorities). This last problem reflects three fundamental problems: (i) excessive legislation, (ii) inadequate decentralization of authority as far as interpretations are concerned, (iii) inadequate services to taxpayers with regard to tax information (Ministry of Economy and Labour Affairs 2004).

Apart from the barriers related to starting a business, barriers to developing a business are also significant. They include market barriers (problems with identifying market demand), social insurance (among other things, mandatory social insurance contributions paid on workers' behalf to the government, restrictions on laying off/terminating employees), financial barriers (access to financing and cost of financing), legal barriers (transparency, equal treatment of entities, proper application, effectiveness), information (availability of information) and infrastructural (telecommunication, transport) barriers. Other important factors include poor management, insufficient cooperation with other companies, weak collaboration with research and development (R&D) units, rare contacts with advisory and technical agencies and with financial institutions, and a lack of aid from external institutions.

As well as these numerous barriers, it is also necessary to take into account the continuing use of methods inherited from a centrally-planned economy, and an inadequate level of initiative and entrepreneurship in company management. Other difficulties include a lack of or difficult access to capital, while high interest rates on loans actually deter any bold ventures. Lack of positive experience available to many generations of old Western companies discourages initiatives aimed at creating sophisticated, innovative enterprises, capable of competing on domestic and international markets. All of the above-mentioned conditions notwithstanding, a great number of enterprises were established in Poland on the basis of already existing factories, or as a result of individual creativity and entrepreneurial initiatives. One such example is the Kozera company.

COMPETITIVENESS AND INNOVATIVENESS OF POLAND'S SMES

Despite all these difficulties, Polish private companies, including SMEs, were rated favourably by the European Commission in its 'Opinion' of the Polish EU accession application (UKIE 1997). According to the Opinion, in the section on industry competitiveness, Poland's economy was marked by a dichotomy between the good performance of the private sector, dominated by SMEs, and the poor performance of large enterprises, most of which were still state-owned.

This, however, did not prevent SMEs from being generally suspicious of the new circumstances (new opportunities as well as new threats, mostly dependent on external conditions, including the sensitivity of individual companies and sectors to the Single Market programme and their ability to adapt to changing conditions) in which they found themselves after EU accession (Rogut 2002).

EU membership provided Polish producers with full access to the EU market. Even though they had already been able to benefit from the lifting of tariff barriers, at least in relation to most industrial goods,[3] as of 1 May 2004 they were able to take full advantage of the complete eradication of physical, technical and fiscal barriers.[4] Other positive events were the incorporation of Poland into the Common Trade Policy (changing trade terms with third countries) and Common Agricultural Policy (changing the terms of access of Polish agricultural and food products to the EU market).

Experience gained so far in the field of integration demonstrates that Polish SMEs are doing very well in the Single Market, which was evidenced by polls carried out among the owners and managers of SMEs in 2003 to

2005. The very first poll, undertaken six months prior to integration, showed that 35 per cent of interviewees believed that integration with the EU would slightly or considerably undermine the position of their firms (Tokaj-Krzewska and Żolnierski 2004). In the next two polls the percentage of such respondents decreased, falling to 15 per cent at the end of 2004 (Polish Agency for Enterprise Development 2004), and to 14 per cent in December 2005 (Tokaj-Krzewska and Pyciński 2006). A persistent weakness of the Polish SME sector is that companies are still overly attached to short-lived, lower-level advantages (such as lower labour costs), while underestimating investments in higher-level advantages (such as product differentiation, type of customer relationship, saturation with know-how and so on). It is these latter advantages that will have a decisive, long-term influence on the ultimate balance of integration-related benefits. Building these advantages is a derivative of the level of innovativeness, perceived as the ability and motivation to seek and put to commercial use any results of scientific research, new concepts, ideas and inventions in order to increase the level of sophistication of the company and to enhance its competitive position, or in order to implement the technical ambitions of the entrepreneur. That, in turn, is generally very low, which became apparent from a study of the level of innovativeness of Polish SMEs and, speaking more broadly, of Poland's economy as a whole, commissioned by the National Strategy of Cohesion for the years 2007–13 and for the Sectoral Operational Programmes (Ministry of Regional Development 2006). The study notes that although the share of innovative enterprises[5] has recently grown, it still remains considerably lower than the EU average, which has reached 51 per cent.

This diagnosis is fully borne out by the results of the most comprehensive studies of the level of innovativeness carried out in Poland by the Central Statistical Office (Central Statistical Office 2006a). In the years 2002–04 the average share of innovative enterprises reached 25.6 per cent, 8.5 per cent higher than in the years 1998–2000. However, this average was mainly shaped by highly innovative activities in foreign-owned companies, of which more than 38 per cent indicated product and/or process innovation. Such assessment of the level of innovativeness of Polish enterprises is reflected in the low value of the Summary Innovation Index[6] (SII), which resulted in the classification of Poland in 2005 into a group of countries 'losing ground' in terms of innovativeness (TrendChart 2005). The time necessary for Poland to catch up with the rest of Europe in the field of innovations is assessed at a minimum of 50 years (European Innovation Scoreboard 2005). This, in turn, will require the reduction of (at least some) of the barriers identified by SMEs as most onerous to the innovative process.

The results of the Innobarometer 2004 study are a little more optimistic. It only covers companies which have recent (that is, in the last two years) experience of innovative activities[7] (EOS Gallup Europe 2004). In this case Polish companies rank among the leaders in Europe.

It seems, however, inappropriate to blame this state of affairs entirely on SMEs, as the competitiveness of companies in general, and SMEs in particular, is built mainly upon the strength and effectiveness of the national economy,[8] its technical infrastructure and other factors on which external effects depend.

It is a fact that in the last decades radical transformations have taken place (Lipowski 1997; Balcerowicz 1997). The current production structure is reckoned to place Poland somewhere between the north and south of Europe (Weber et al. 1999). However, the most striking weakness is the limited development of high-tech industries (Central Statistical Office 2005). For this reason, Poland is deemed to represent a bi-polar model of structural adaptation, where we can see a fast development of traditional, labour-intensive and related sectors (created by specialized suppliers), side by side with relatively weak results in high-tech sectors.

This illustrates the notion of taking advantage of backwardness, in which countries such as Poland, which at the beginning of their transformation displayed a large gap in productivity and product quality, exploit their high potential for catching-up (Landesmann 2003). An important role in this process is played by foreign direct investment (FDI), as evidenced in Poland by the motor industry, production of electric machines and appliances, production of radio, TV, and telecommunications equipment, production of wood and wood products, and in the furniture and paper industries (Polish Information and Foreign Investment Agency 2006). All these products represent the mid-technology sector, where manufacturing is relatively labour intensive, and where Poland still has an advantage over Western European countries, although it cannot compete with China. Poland benefits in this case from its geographical location (proximity to main European markets, reducing transport costs).

The sort of foreign investment mentioned above is characteristic of the pan-European process of restructuring industry, causing a shift of business operations from EU15 to EU10.[9] This shift is characterized by a certain pattern, according to which it is mainly assembly operations that are moved to EU10, while R&D units remain within EU15 (Halve 2000; European Commission 2001; Midelfart-Knarvik et al. 2003; Economic Policy Committee 2003; Jungmittag 2004; Duszczyk et al. 2005; UKIE 2006). There do exist, however, certain surveys confirming the possibility of reversing these tendencies (United Nations 2005).

BREAKING BARRIERS: KOZERA CASE STUDY

A Short History of the Kozera Company

The owner of the company, Mieczysław Kozera, is now 54 years old. He graduated from the Foundry Technical High School in Koluszki, while working at the Wifama textile factory in Łódź. In 1974, he participated in the preparations for the launching of a new foundry of non-ferrous metals – Zakłady Urządzeń Klimatyzacyjnych Uniprot in Łódź. A year later he was promoted to the position of shift supervisor, and then to the position of foundry technologist. He won the title 'Young Champion of Technology' three times. He also owns three patents and industrial designs. He believes that his stamina and will to overcome difficulties come from his time spent as a representative of the Polish Army in the Olimp Złocieniec soccer team and as a competitive long-distance runner. He is also a keen angler and traveller. For his active promotion of tourism, Kozera was awarded the Golden Badge of the PTTK.[10] In 2000, Łódź entrepreneurs elected him as the Chairman of the Chamber of Industry and Commerce in Łódź. The President of the Republic of Poland has awarded him the Silver Cross of Merit for his services for the development of local authorities.

The history of his firm dates back to 1981, when Mieczysław Kozera, then a thirty-year-old foundryman professional, lost his job after martial law was imposed. He borrowed approximately 100 000 PLN (€25 000) from his brother and some other family members to establish a store in Łódź selling ceramic and glass products (for instance, artistic glass, which used to be very popular) and household appliances. High demand for such goods supported the development of his company, and in 1989 he decided to acquire the bankrupt rubber plant Przedsiębiorstwo Wyrobów Gumowych Stomil in Lutomiersk, a small town of some 2000 inhabitants on the Ner river, 18 kilometres from the provincial capital of Łódź.

Kozera was not interested in producing rubber goods. He purchased the plant with the view to adapting the buildings into a small glassware factory. Because, as a foundryman he knew little about the production of glass goods, he decided to hire some employees from glassworks in Krosno and Szklarska Poręba, towns located hundreds of kilometres away from Lutomiersk.

Bank Rzemiosła in Łódź granted him a loan for the purchase of the production facilities. These assets were used to buy machines and appliances from bankrupt glassware factories. This enabled Przedsiębiorstwo Kozera to launch the production of artistic glassware.

Meanwhile, Kozera noticed a rapid rise in demand for ceramic garden products. As the standard of living for much of the Polish population improved, people became more interested in beautifying their homes, cottages and gardens. Identifying this growing market niche, in 1992 the company acquired one hectare of land for the construction of a ceramics factory. Basic machinery was acquired from Bomis, a company specializing in the acquisition of machines and appliances from bankrupt factories. The payments were made in instalments. The company purchased 18 furnaces with the capacity of one cubic metre each. More equipment was purchased from former public companies which had over-invested in machinery and were unable to pay taxes for underutilized machines. Thus, the company managed to purchase special mills from the porcelain factory Fabryki Porcelany in Jaworzno and filtration presses and moulds from a plant in Tłuszcz. The investment process was concluded in 1996. At that time, the company was employing 100 people. Encouraged by the company's success, the owner decided to diversify its operations into new business areas.

Among other things, he opened a petrol station. It required a substantial investment in construction, purchasing tanker lorries and so on, but at the same time it gave high returns. With the growth of the number of new companies, demand for means of transport, and consequently for fuel, spiralled. Thousands of lorries were imported for start-up companies, as well as passenger cars both for company and private use. Entering the fuel market guaranteed a financial success.

The Kozera company was the first in Poland to open a private petrol station in Lutomiersk, followed by more stations in Sieradz, Konstantynów and Łódź. Some time later, in 1997, a wholesale fuel delivery operation was launched – such an unusual initiative at that time that the company's success was widely covered by radio, TV and newspapers. In addition, Kozera started to manufacture furniture, furniture fittings and furniture accessories. Profits generated from fuel sales were invested in the development of furniture centres and the glassware factory. In 1999, a ceramics and glassware manufacturing plant was built on a five-hectare plot; the plant had a floor area of 8000 square metres and employed 350 people.

Despite its best efforts, the Kozera company was not able to ensure highly qualified technical and production staff for its glassware factory. The clients' expectations regarding both the quality and design increased. Professionals from other localities were not interested in relocation to Lutomiersk. Following a hasty decision taken by the educational authorities to close down secondary technical schools, the availability of qualified technical staff diminished. In such a situation, the absence of tradition, and consequently lack of professional and experienced personnel forced the company to cease the production of artistic glassware in 2003. The company disposed of part of its machinery retaining only those machines useful for the production of garden pots, such as machines for manufacturing glaze. Some machines were sold to employees who decided to open their own businesses with the assistance of the Kozera company. This decision brought savings on production costs and enabled the purchase of modern production lines from the Italian company Fuccelli for the manufacture of garden pots and to launch the production of garden figures. Kozera decided that his workers' skills, as well as his own competence and experience in the ceramic products sector, constituted an excellent basis for a further development of manufacturing ceramic products.

Company Organization and Market Share

The Kozera company belongs to a group of companies (owned by Mr Kozera) which are unafraid to diversify their business activities, never hesitating to give up operations in any sector that ceases to yield the expected level of income. After ceasing the production of artistic glassware, the company re-entered the market as a supplier of fuel, furniture boards and finished furniture. The recreation centre in the seaside resort of Sianorzęty, also owned by the Kozera company, inspired Mr Kozera to move into hotel services sector. At present, the company is building a hotel in Łódź with 100 rooms and 180 beds. Also, a shopping and service centre will be commissioned with a floor area of 4000 square metres, offering food, industrial and gardening products.

The Kozera company is a sole trader and its organizational structure is very simple (Figure 8.1), but effective and clear to employees. Mr Kozera functions as a one-man management board, supervising the marketing and market cooperation department, the ceramics plant, the shopping and service centre, and the fuel trading plant. He is helped by an assistant,

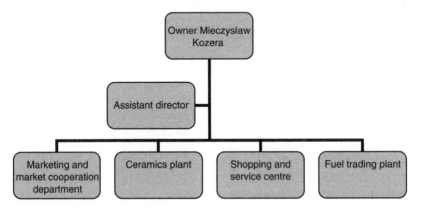

Source: Firm's documentation.

Figure 8.1   Organizational graph of the Kozera company

whose responsibilities include keeping in touch with external companies providing human relations (HR), occupational health and safety, and bookkeeping services. He also prepares documents necessary for carrying out business talks and price negotiations.

The marketing and market cooperation department develops strategies to be applied in individual markets and tests market demand. The department employs six graphic artists, designing new products. This is also where decisions are taken on participation in domestic and foreign trade fairs, exhibitions and advertising campaigns. The marketing department is also responsible for taking orders and transferring them to relevant plants. Moreover, it is kept informed on the quality of products, as it incorporates a quality laboratory. Visitors are often surprised at these extensive responsibilities. However, both the staff and the owner claim that this guarantees the ability to react immediately to market needs, and serves the purpose of building effective customer relationships. Human resources and bookkeeping services are outsourced to specialist institutions. The same principle applies to occupational health and safety. As an additional benefit, the company has gained access to independent labour safety audits. The company also maintains a repairs and construction team of four employees, whose tasks include keeping the company in good technical condition. More complicated works, associated with machine repairs or construction works, are outsourced to specialist companies.

Since 2000, the company has been running a strict policy of production and employment restructuring, getting rid of unnecessary machines and appliances, as well as of inefficient production processes and work stations. Apart from efficient management, the lean structure enables the company to achieve good performance levels.

At present (2006), the company employs 160 staff members, compared to two employed in the initial period of the company's activity, and as many as 370 people in 2000. However, since that time, employment has been gradually reduced. Employment levels were reduced naturally, that is, by way of restructuring the firm and stimulating business creation and entrepreneurship. Such was the case of the repair and construction plant, the artistic glassware plant and the fuel stations (leased to employees).

The company's largest customer is Russia, where 50 per cent of its entire sales volume is generated. Other markets include France, the Czech Republic, Germany, Ukraine, Slovakia, Belarus, Lithuania and Austria.

Competitiveness and Innovativeness of Kozera

In its present form, Kozera is Poland's leading manufacturer of clay pots and garden statues. However, most of the production is exported, and only

15 per cent is sold on the domestic market. Domestic buyers are mostly large chain stores, but the company also sells to multinational corporations such as Obi, Tesco, Leclerc, Praktiker, Castorama, Bricco, Real, Nomi and a small group of specialist gardening stores. After Poland's accession to the European Union, along with other Polish companies, Kozera was forced to undergo a crash course on competitiveness and ability to compete on the Single Market. The company first gained international experience by exporting its products to the mature markets of the EU 15 as well as to Russia and Ukraine. This experience, in turn, was decisive for subsequent changes in the technology and technique of production and for subordinating decision-making to market requirements and customer suggestions. Participation in domestic and foreign trade fairs, as well as cooperation with numerous production and trading companies provided Kozera with abundant opportunities to apply conscious benchmarking and to transfer best practices. The first areas of change included the organization of order-taking and commissioning production, eliminating high-cost recipients, supply and sales logistics, transportation (for instance, the Schencker Company) and outsourcing a number of functions.

By investing in the most sophisticated technologies and appropriate equipment for the production of ceramic pots and figures, Kozera became the largest manufacturer in the country, capable of competing with Western companies.

The company's major competitors are suppliers from China, who have won a considerable market share by offering low prices for their products. Kozera's competitive advantages include prompt reaction to the customers' needs, fast implementation, production, and realization of orders, timing of deliveries and good quality, as well as design which often draws on the folklore, fauna and flora of the client's country. Kozera gains further substantial competitive advantage over its competitors from China because it is capable of producing small quantities to order in a short period of time reducing delivery time and the risk related to ordering an excessive quantity of goods, and eliminating high shipment costs for the client. With this philosophy of being open to the customers' needs and benefits, the Kozera company continues to gain additional clients within the European Union.

The company identifies Portugal as its most serious competitor in manufacturing ceramic products in the European Union. In response, Kozera employs well-educated and experienced designers who prepare original and unique designs that are an important asset in the competitive struggle. Several thousand designs and patterns owned by the company are displayed in a special design hall, including descriptions and catalogue cards, which, if need be, may be printed on the spot. The company's most recent 'market hit' are garden pots and statues made of terracotta that is strong enough to survive the winter outdoors.

Additionally, Kozera intends to promote a centre for garden ceramics and artistic glass in Lutomiersk, which is popular with the people of Łódź as an attractive place to visit and to buy inexpensive artistic glass and ceramics as well as blacksmith products from local artists. The town of Lutomiersk is widely associated in Poland with these kind of products. The Kozera company is the largest manufacturing enterprise in the town (the production capacity is planned to grow to 200 000 products per month, up from the current level of 80 000), supported by 15 micro-enterprises established earlier thanks to the support and technical assistance of the Kozera company.

Another element supporting the competitiveness of the company is its unlimited access to domestic raw materials, such as the right type of clay, dyes and glazing material. The entire production cycle is closed, without any waste products. Broken or inadequate products eliminated by quality control are directed to special dustless mills (so-called wet mills) and recycled back into the production process. The ecologically clean manufacturing methods are approved by the inhabitants of Lutomiersk, who support the company's further development. In the course of the last five years, the company allocated nearly 40 per cent of its income to the implementation of innovative solutions and the procurement of new machines and technologies. So far, despite submitting applications for assistance from EU funds supporting the development of enterprise competitiveness, the company has never been granted any funding of that kind.

Participation in trade fairs and exhibitions provides an excellent opportunity to present the company's achievements. In 2000, 2001 and 2002, the company was awarded gold medals at the Interflat and Inerglass trade fairs in Łódź and in 2005 it received a gold medal at the Cwiety–Kwiaty flower exhibition in Moscow. Such distinctions enhance the company's image and help it build its competitive advantages.

In its diversification, Kozera relies on well-established operations, using the market experience collected by the company and its staff. A good example of this approach is the development of hotel services. The decision to build a hotel in Łódź responds to the needs of the city, which is not only a provincial capital, but an important centre for international fairs, exhibitions, conferences and symposia. As Mr Kozera said 'it would be a mistake not to make use of the knowledge and skills of the staff, and take advantage of the opportunity to offer hotel services in Łódź, which is still a developing city'. This new business is based on his experience from the services offered in the former seaside centre in Sianorzęty.

Another innovative project is the implementation of the company's own training programme for technical and shop-floor staff. It provides education in the field of modelling and the construction of ceramic products, glazing, painting ceramics, and different methods of firing. In the course of the programme, the employees learn both about the construction of machines and how to operate them. Information about the functioning of the Kozera company and the rights and duties of both employees and the company constitutes an important part of the training programme. The project provides the company with adequately trained personnel, thus compensating for the lack of secondary technical training.

In order to ensure a constant inflow of qualified personnel, Kozera is also planning to open a professional training centre, where employees of the company and other producers and distributors of ceramic goods and their sales personnel could learn how to make models and ornaments, form and fire ceramic products, and operate furnaces and other appliances used in the production of ceramics. Participants from outside Lódź will be able to use the company's accommodation. Relevant technical and scientific staff are easily available, as Lódź is an important Polish academic centre.

CONCLUSIONS

Had it not been for the situation in which he found himself after being dismissed from work, Mr Kozera would probably still be an ordinary worker in a state-owned enterprise. Although he had neither money, nor proper technical background, nor support from state structures, he was assisted in his entrepreneurial endeavours by experience gained in the field of production rationalization and people skills. Financial support from his close relatives was also very important. This enabled him to take advantage of the opportunity created by changes in Polish legislation, which were slowly removing the barriers that used to slow down the pace of development of Polish private companies.

Initially, the obstacles that Mr Kozera faced were a generally negative attitude towards entrepreneurs and the corruption of officials at various levels. A stereotype shared by the vast majority of Polish society is that of the entrepreneur as a 'capitalist' engaged in unfair financial activities and tax evasion and who avoids paying his employees. Such is the image of the entrepreneur portrayed by the mass media. The situation was particularly difficult for SMEs because since 1950 entrepreneurs had had no organization capable of defending them and representing their interests to the local and central administration. In such an environment, Mr Kozera, like many other entrepreneurs, had not only to have entrepreneurial skills, but also resilience and self-confidence, and a readiness to stand up for his rights and to take risks. However, these remain characteristic of successful entrepreneurs even today; in the initial stage of transformation they were indispensable for the creation and development of a business.

Other factors contributing to Mr Kozera's success were his ability to see and make use of opportunities and to build competitive advantages. As he says himself, in the case of his company, innovativeness is 'a result of my curiosity and my will to learn how other people work and what they need, and eventually if I can offer them what they need'.

Another source of Mr Kozera's success is access to good information. 'Taking advantage of my colleagues' experience, I learned how to strengthen my position in negotiations with the supermarkets and shopping centres. When I was considering closing the glassware factory, I understood the very basic principle of business: you should not undertake any actions just to satisfy your ambitions, the goal of an entrepreneur should be the satisfaction of the needs of his clients. If this still does not bring you any satisfaction, you have to look further for your place in business.'

The competitiveness and innovativeness of the Kozera company were further enhanced by Mr Kozera's participation in the activities of the Chamber of Industry and Commerce. As he says, 'the work in the Chamber gave me the opportunity to meet national and international businessmen'. Special emphasis is put on the reduction of transaction costs by access to information, participation in business missions and meetings, as well as enhancing purchasing power by maintaining contacts with chain stores.

NOTES

1. Given the population of nearly 38 157 000 at the end of 2005, this means almost 94 firms per 1000 inhabitants.
2. The TEA index is essentially the sum of all nascent entrepreneurs (people in the process of starting a new business) and new businesses. For more information see Acs et al. (2005).
3. Which was the subject of the European Agreement establishing Poland's association with the European Communities and their member states as well as of agreements on trading industrial products within free-trade zones. This was the case with former CEFTA member states as well as with Lithuania, Latvia, and Estonia. In the case of Cyprus and Malta, trade was regulated by clauses of the most-favoured-nation status, which ensured that partners must not be treated any worse than the most favoured country.
4. Physical, technical, and fiscal barriers are three basic types of barriers specified by the EU White Paper in the matter of completing the building of the single market (Commission of the European Communities 1985).
5. That is, companies which have implemented innovations over the past three years (TrendChart 2005).
6. SII uses two types of indices: an index of investment in innovation, and an index of innovation results. The index of investment in innovation is comprised of three sub-indices (1) innovation motors; (2) production of knowledge; (3) innovation and entrepreneurship. The index of innovation results comprise two sub-indices: (1) application; (2) intellectual property. For a detailed description of the SII methodology see Sajeva et al. (2005).

7. Innovation activities were defined as a wide range of activities to improve the firm's performance, including the implementation of a new or significantly improved product, service, distribution process, manufacturing process, marketing method or organizational method (EOS Gallup Europe 2004).
8. The subject is thoroughly discussed in, among others, Council of Ministers (2006), Ministry of Regional Development (2006), Ministry of Economy (2006), Ministry of Economy and Labour Affairs (2004).
9. New member states.
10. Polskie Towarzystwo Turystyczno Krajoznawcze, Polish Tourist Country Lovers' Society, a registered public charity integrating a tourist movement and rural country lovers, actively protecting the natural environment and taking care of monuments.

REFERENCES

Acs, Z.J., P. Arenius, M. Hay and M. Minniti (2005), *Global Entrepreneurship Monitor. 2004 Executive Report*, Babson College and London Business School.
Audretsch, D.B. (2003), 'Entrepreneurship: A Survey of the Literature', Enterprise Papers No. 4, Luxembourg: Office for Official Publications of the European Communities.
Bacławski, K., M. Koczerga and P. Zabierowski (2005), *Studium przedsiębiorczości w Polsce w roku 2004. Raport GEM Polska*, Poznań: Fundacja Edukacyjna Bachalski.
Balcerowicz, L. (1997), *Socjalizm. Kapitalizm. Transformacja. Szkice z przełomu epok*, Warsaw: Wydawnictwo Naukowe PWN.
Central Statistical Office (2005), *Nauka i technika w 2003 r.*, Warsaw.
Central Statistical Office (2006a), *Działalność innowacyjna przedsiębiorstw przemysłowych w latach 2002–2004*, Warsaw.
Central Statistical Office (2006b), *Podmioty gospodarcze według rodzajów i miejsc prowadzenia działalności w 2005 r.*, Warsaw.
Commission of the European Communities (1985), *Completing the Internal Market*, White Paper from the Commission to the European Council (Milan, 28–29 June), COM (85) 310 final, Brussels.
Council of Ministers (2005), 'Projekt Narodowego Planu Rozwoju 2007–2013', www.npr.gov.pl, accessed 10 September 2006.
Council of Ministers (2006), 'Projekt Narodowego Planu Rozwoju 2007–2013', www.npr.gov.pl, accessed 10 September 2006.
Duszczyk, M., M. Budzyńska, A. Byrt, M. Gancarz, E. Gieroczyńska, M. Jatczak, M. Kałużyńska, A. Rotuska and K. Wójcik (2005), *Wybrane aspekty konkurencyjności europejskiej. Stan debaty*, Warsaw: Office of the Committee for European Integration.
Dzierżanowski, W. and M. Stachowiak (eds) (2001), *Report on the Condition of SMEs in Poland in the Years 1999–2000*, Warsaw: Polish Agency for Enterprise Development.
EBRD (2006), 'Poland: EBRD Country Factsheet', www.ebrd.org/pubs/factsh/country/poland.pdf, accessed 13 January 2007.
Economic Policy Committee (2003), 'Key Structural Challenges in the Acceding Countries: The Integration of the Acceding Countries into the Community's Economic Policy Co-ordination Processes', Occasional Papers No. 4, www.europa.eu.int/comm/economy, accessed 15 August 2006.

EOS Gallup Europe (2004), Flash Eurobarometer 164. Innobarometer 2004, ec.europa.eu/public_opinion/archives/flash_arch_en.htm, accessed 25 June 2005.

Etemad, H. (2004), 'International Entrepreneurship as a Dynamic Adaptive System: Towards a Grounded Theory', *Journal of International Entrepreneurship*, **2**, 5–59.

European Commission (2001), *Real Convergence in Candidate Countries – Past Performance and Scenarios in the Pre-Accession Economic Programmes*, ECFIN/708/01-EN, Brussels: European Commission Directorate General Economic and Financial Affairs.

Halve, P. (2000), 'Trade and Cost Competitiveness in the Czech Republic, Hungary, Poland, and Slovenia', World Bank Technical paper No. 482, Washington: World Bank.

Jungmittag, A. (2004), 'Innovations, Technological Specialization and Economic Growth in the EU', European Economy, Economic Papers No. 199, www. europa.eu.int/comm./economy_finance, accessed 17 September 2006.

Kirzner, I.M. (1979), *Perception, Opportunity and Profit*, Chicago: University of Chicago Press.

Landesmann, M.A. (2003), 'Structural Features of Economic Integration in an Enlarged Europe: Patterns of Catching-Up and Industrial Specialization', European Economy, Economic Papers No. 181, europa.eu.int/comm./economy_ finance, accessed 14 November 2004.

Lipowski, A. (1997), 'Przezwyciężenie dysproporcji w strukturze produkcji przemysłowej', in M. Belka and W. Trzeciakowski (eds), *Dynamika transformacji polskiej gospodarki*, Warsaw: Poltext, pp. 143–70.

Midelfart-Knarvik, K.H., H.G. Overman, S.J. Redding and A.J. Venables (2003), 'The Location of European Industry', in *European Integration and the Functioning of Product Markets*, Special report No. 2/2002, Brussels: European Economy, European Commission Directorate-General for Economic and Financial Affairs, pp. 213–70.

Ministry of Economy (2006), 'Kierunki zwiększania innowacyjności gospodarki na lata 2007–2013', www.mg.gov.pl, accessed 28 April 2006.

Ministry of Economy and Labour Affairs (2004), 'Inwestycyjny proces budowlany. Bariery inwestycyjne oraz propozycje działań usprawniających', www.mgip. gov.pl, accessed 25 September 2006.

Ministry of Regional Development (2006), 'Polska. Narodowe Strategiczne Ramy Odniesienia 2007–2013 wspierające wzrost gospodarczy i zatrudnienie', Preliminary Draft, Document approved by the Council of Ministers on 14 February 2006, www.mrr.gov.pl, accessed 13 January 2007.

Piasecki, B. (1997), *Przedsiębiorczość i mała firma. Teoria i praktyka*, Lódź: Wydawnictwo Uniwersytetu tŁódzkiego.

Polish Agency for Enterprise Development (2004), 'Raport z badania sondażowego wśród małych i średnich firm w Polsce, Opinia', www.parp.gov.pl, accessed 25 September 2006.

Polish Information and Foreign Investment Agency (2003), *Polska rajem dla inwestorów? Bariery inwestycyjne w Polsce oraz propozycje rozwiązań ukierunkowanych na ich usuwanie*, Warsaw.

Polish Information and Foreign Investment Agency (2006), *Lista największych inwestorów zagranicznych w Polsce*, Warsaw.

Rogut, A. (2002), *Małe i średnie przedsiębiorstwa w integracji europejskiej. Doświadczenia Unii Europejskiej. Lekcje dla Polski*, Łódź: Wydawnictwo Uniwersytetu Łódzkiego.

Sajeva, M., D. Gatelli, S. Tarantola and H. Hollanders (2005), 'Methodology Report on European Innovation Scoreboard 2005', *European Trend Chart on Innovation*, www.trendchart.org, accessed 17 September 2006.

Tokaj-Krzewska, A. and A. Żołnierski (eds) (2004), *Report on the Condition of SMEs in Poland in the Years 2002–2003*, Warsaw: Ministry of Economy and Labour Affairs, Polish Agency for Enterprise Development.

Tokaj-Krzewska, A. and S. Pyciński (eds) (2006), *Report on the Condition of SMEs in Poland in the Years 2004–2005*, Warsaw: Polish Agency for Enterprise Development.

TrendChart (2005), European Innovation Scoreboard, Comparative Analysis of Innovation Performance. European Trend Chart on Innovation, www.trendchart. org, accessed 17 September 2006.

UKIE (1997), 'Agenda 2000. Opinion of the European Commission on Poland's application for membership in the European Union', *Monitor Integracji Europejskiej*, Special Issue, Warsaw: Office of the Committee for European Integration.

UKIE (2006), *Delokalizacja w rozszerzonej Unii Europejskiej. perspektywa wybranych państw UE. Wnioski dla Polski*, Warsaw: Office of the Committee for European Integration.

United Nations (2005), *World Investment Report 2005. Transnational Corporations and the Internationalization of R&D*, New York and Geneva: United Nations Conference on Trade and Development.

Weber, M., W. Meske and K. Ducatel (1999), *The Wider Picture. Enlargement and Cohesion in Europe*, Seville: European Commission, Institute for Prospective Technological Studies.

World Bank (2005), *Doing Business in 2005. Removing Obstacles to Growth*, Washington: The International Bank for Reconstruction and Development/The World Bank.

9. Seaway: building boats in Slovenia

Daniel Shapiro, Aleš Vahčič and Lisa Papania

INTRODUCTION

Entrepreneurial activity, the capacity to create and sustain new businesses, has been a challenge for emerging and transition economies, but is at the same time critical for their success (McMillan and Woodruff 2002). The main feature of the environment in transition countries is the movement from a system based on planning to one based on markets. Even though most transition economies did contain some privately owned firms, even before liberalization, the environment for entrepreneurship has been characterized as 'hostile' (Smallbone and Welter 2001). Although there are various factors that contribute to this, most result from the absence of well-functioning markets and supportive market institutions (Khanna et al. 2005; Khanna and Rivkin 2001). Market failures in emerging and transition markets not only limit opportunities, but are associated with problems in raising capital and with finding appropriate human and physical capital, or more generally in acquiring necessary complementary resources (Meyer and Peng 2005; Aidis 2005). Despite these obstacles, successful entrepreneurial firms do emerge.

Seaway, a Slovenian company, is one of the world's leading developers of sailing boats and powerboats, engaged in the end-to-end production process from design, engineering, and tooling, to the manufacture of components. The company was founded by two brothers, Japec and Jernej Jakopin as a boat design company in 1989. Today, the company sells its products and services globally, and is currently the leading producer of sailing boat rudders and bearings. Its competitive advantage is, in part, based on its design and innovation capabilities, for which it has won numerous international awards, and which have enabled it to grow into a profitable mid-size producer of luxury boats. The company is expected to attain a market value of €100 to 150 million in three to five years, at which stage it will likely either go public, or be acquired.

In order to analyse the particular case of Seaway, we adopt the approach suggested by Shane and Venkataraman (2000) and extended by Baker et al. (2005). Shane and Venkataraman (2000) argue that entrepreneurial activity involves the discovery, evaluation and exploitation of available opportunities. As such, understanding entrepreneurial activity requires an understanding of the sources of opportunities, the process by which they are discovered, the way they are exploited, and the nature of the individuals who engage in discovery and exploitation. Thus, understanding entrepreneurial activity requires an understanding of both the individual(s) who are involved and the environment in which they operate.

Accordingly, Seaway's success is illustrated in terms of the political and economic environment in Slovenia, and the talents and skills of the brothers that enabled them to overcome the challenges that they faced. As we discuss, although Slovenia is in some senses not a classic transition economy, it nevertheless poses considerable challenges to entrepreneurial activity. Thus, Seaway is a case study that highlights the obstacles that start-ups face in many emerging and transition markets. We will discuss these obstacles and indicate the ways in which specific aspects of the Slovenian environment and the personal characteristics of the founders combined to create a globally successful firm. We will focus in particular on the role of financing, the importance of links to related institutions, including the university, and the characteristics of the founders.

SLOVENIA

Slovenia is a small country of only 2 million people, but it also has the highest GDP per capita of any transition economy in Eastern Europe, nearly 80 per cent of the EU average (Economist Intelligence Unit 2006). Compared with other transition economies in the region, it has achieved a relatively high degree of macroeconomic stability, with low rates of inflation and unemployment (Table 9.1).

The political history of Slovenia contributed significantly to its development. Originally a part of Austria, Slovenia became part of Yugoslavia when that country was formed in 1929. In 1945, under communist leadership, it was made a republic of Yugoslavia. The communist system in Yugoslavia was fairly liberal. From 1958, citizens were issued with passports and allowed to exit and enter the country freely. In 1968, citizens were permitted to open foreign exchange accounts, and to legally withdraw foreign currencies and deposit funds earned outside Yugoslavia. Thus, relative to other transition economies, Slovenia experienced more foreign exposure.

Business was also relatively liberalized, with firms able to choose where and in which companies to invest. Limitations on new ventures imposed by the government included the right of the communist party to choose a

Table 9.1 *General information: Slovenia and selected transition economies*

	Bulgaria	Czech R.	Estonia	Hungary	Latvia	Lithuania	Poland	Romania	Slovak R.	Slovenia
Population in millions	7.8	10.2	1.4	10.1	2.3	3.4	38.2	21.7	5.4	2
Area ('000 sq. km)	111	78.9	45	93	64.5	67	313.9	238	49	20.5
GDP (in billion US$ 2004)	24.1	107	11.2	100.3	13.5	22.3	241.8	73.2	41.1	32.2
GDP per cap in 2004 at current international US$ (PPP)	8 026	19 311	13 740	16 596	11 962	12 994	12 876	8 413	14 549	20 853
Private sector share in GDP (%) in 2005	70	80	80	80	70	75	75	70	80	65
Inflation 2005 estimation (%)	4.2	2	3.9	3.8	6.4	2.8	2.2	9.2	2.4	2.5
Unemployment rate (UNECE 2003)	13.6	7.8	10.1	5.8	10.5	12.7	19.2	6.6	17.1	6.5
FDI inflows (as a % of GDP) 2004	5.1	3.7	7	3.6	4	2.3	2	3.1	1	3.3

Sources: EBRD (2005); UNECE for unemployment rates (www.unece.org).

firm's management team. This applied to any business with more than five employees. Enterprises consisting of fewer than five members were considered entrepreneurial ventures, and given the freedom to operate independently.

Today, Slovenia ranks relatively highly on the World Bank Doing Business Indicators (Table 9.2), when compared with other transition economies in Europe. In particular, it appears to be somewhat more attractive in terms of the costs and licences involved with starting a business, although the time required does take longer. Hiring workers is relatively easy, although firing them is somewhat harder.

An academic career was always attractive in Slovenia. Even under communism, professors were not required to be party members, despite the concentration of intellectually powerful people in universities. Perhaps as a consequence, Slovenia has a tradition of academic excellence, and its performance in R&D and patenting is above the average of other transition countries in Europe (Table 9.3).

Historically, the political environment attached high social status to academics and professionals, but limited the ability of companies to function independently of the state. Overcoming these obstacles was the domain of individuals who exhibited a particular combination of characteristics, including social status, intelligence, international knowledge, and business

Table 9.2   World Bank Doing Business Indicators: Slovenia and transition economies

	Slovenia	Region[a]	OECD
Starting a business (% per cap income)	9.4	14.1	5.3
Dealing with licences (% per cap income)	122.2	564.9	72
Hiring workers (% salary)	16.6	26.7	21.4
Firing costs (weeks of wages)	39.6	26.2	31.3
Registering property (% property value)	2	2.7	4.3
Public credit registry coverage (% adults)	2.9	1.7	8.4
Total tax rate (% profit)	39.4	56	47.8
Enforcing a contract (% debt)	15.2	15	11.2
Closing a business (% estate)	8	14.3	7.1
Time required to start a business (days)	61	41.4	n.a
Market capitalization of listed companies (% of GDP)	25.7	23.9	n.a

Note: a. Region = Bulgaria, Czech Republic, Estonia, Hungary, Latvia, Lithuania, Poland, Romania and Slovakia.

Source: World Bank (2006).

Table 9.3   R&D in Slovenia and selected transition economies

	Transition countries (average)	Slovenia	EU 15	USA
Public R&D expenditures (% of GDP/year)	0.41	0.63	0.69	0.76
Business R&D expenditures (% of GDP)	0.27	0.9	1.3	2.04
European Patent Office high-tech patent applications	6.48	32.8	31.6	57

Source: European Commission (2005).

acumen. These characteristics, all descriptive of Japec and Jernej Jakopin, were critical to the creation and growth of Seaway.

SEAWAY D.O.O.[1]

In their twenties, Japec Jakopin (a doctor and cardiology researcher) and his brother Jernej (an architect), were skilful amateur yacht builders. In the 1980s, the building of amateur yachts was a popular hobby with the elite of Slovenes who sought to imitate a 'Western' lifestyle. So advanced were the Jakopins' boat-designing abilities that professional boat-building companies, including several in Italy – acknowledged leaders in luxury yacht building – bought licences for their designs.

Consequently, in 1983 the brothers opened the J&J design studio. The prevailing Yugoslav regulatory environment prevented them from expanding their business without state intervention, which frustrated these young entrepreneurs who had left high profile and respected careers in academia and architecture to pursue this venture. However, 1989 saw a regime change in Yugoslavia, and with it, the abolition of these restrictions. The brothers created Seaway d.o.o., of which J&J design studio became a part, and which exceeded the previously state-imposed limit of five employees.

While the local industry was (and is) largely informal and limited, Slovenia was surrounded by advanced yacht-building countries in Europe, including Italy, France, Germany and Scandinavia, and this geographic proximity helped bring the brothers' work to the attention of other boatbuilders. It also enabled Seaway to expand and diversify its offerings, selling nautical equipment, clothes and shoes, through seven ship's chandlers along the Adriatic coast.

However, in 1991, the war for Slovenia's independence forced Seaway to focus on engineering, rather than trade. Seaway was the only independent company outside of the major boat manufacturers that engaged in the entire end-to-end (concept to final mould) production process.

In 1992, Seaway started designing boats for Schoechl, the largest manufacturer of sailing boats in Germany; and also for Bavaria, one of the largest and best boat-building companies in Europe. Seaway added Etap, the largest boat manufacturer in Belgium (1996), Italian manufacturer, Cantiere del Pardoto (1997), and American Outboard Motor Company (1999) to its list of clients. By the turn of the century, over 150 models, and over 44 000 Seaway boats had been produced, and Seaway was known world-wide as a leader in boat design. In 1995, Japec and Jernej were named Entrepreneurs of the Year in Slovenia.

From 1994–2005, revenues had grown from €1.7 million to over €16 million (Table 9.4). The number of employees had increased over that same period from 22 to 120 (Table 9.5). Except for 2001 the company had earned positive profits. However, this expansion and subsequent success brought problems. In 2000 it became apparent that future growth would require the company to manufacture its own moulds and tools with robotic technology, and move beyond design. However, internally generated funds were insufficient to fund the technology and capital expansion was required to enable the company to continue to grow.

Financing Alternatives

In 2000, Seaway's future was called into question. Bavaria complained that Seaway's moulds produced asymmetrical boats in Bavaria's mechanized production process (unlike in a manual process where small inconsistencies could be adjusted). Since 1992, Bavaria had grown from €10 million to 200 million, in large part due to Seaway's designs, to become the second largest manufacturer in Europe. Seaway was hugely dependent on Bavaria's business, but without large investments in technology, was unable to respond to Bavaria's demands. Dismissing the option of applying to lending institutions for money, Seaway considered private funding alternatives.[2]

Seaway needed to buy a robot to produce moulds, but the new equipment required four times more space than Seaway's existing premises offered. A former textile factory was found, but cost €1.5 million, in addition to the €1.5 million for the robot. One option was to form a partnership between Seaway and four European nautical companies (including Bavaria) – whose most successful boats had been designed by Seaway – to become the fourth biggest boat-builder in the world. The deal would be backed by Kmeča

Table 9.4 Seaway: summary income statement, 1994–2005 (€1000)

	1994	1995	1996	1997	1998	1999	2000	2001	2002	2003	2004	2005
Total revenue	1 682	2 134	2 254	2 831	4 918	5 396	6 575	4 311	8 263	8 571	10 719	16 340
Total expenses	1 564	2 123	2 188	2 758	4 790	5 311	5 980	4 402	8 010	7 798	9 937	14 546
Total profit or loss	119	10	66	73	129	84	595	−92	254	773	782	1 794
Taxes	5	9	11	15	16	33	58	0	0	144	0	224
Net profit or loss for the period	112	2	55	58	112	52	537	−92	254	631	782	1 570

Source: Company data.

Table 9.5 *Seaway: selected performance data, 1994–2005*

	1994	1995	1996	1997	1998	1999	2000	2001	2002	2003	2004	2005
Average number of employees	22	24	27	30	39	40	40	38	38	38	83	120
Added value per employee (€1000)	23	25	18	21	24	33	49	27	51	38	30	32
Total revenue per employee (€1000)	98	111	101	112	146	153	180	123	231	235	132	136
Net profit or loss per employee (€1000)	7	0	2	2	3	1	15	−3	7	17	10	13
Return on assets (ROA)	25	0	5	5	8	3	19	−5	6	12	9	12
Return on equity (ROE)	131	1	26	20	27	8	60	−7	9	19	20	30

Source: Company data.

družba (KD), the largest private finance group in Slovenia, and US firm Morgenthaler Ventures. Another option was to cooperate with Elan, a local company and a world leader in the manufacture of skis, which had diversified into boat-building. Neither of these plans materialized, and Seaway continued its search for financing.

In 2001, the Jakopin brothers set up a new company, Seaway Group, and KD directly invested €3 million in Seaway in return for 50 per cent of the company, board representation, and a commitment to a strategy that involved Seaway producing its own boats, and growing from 2.5 million to 5.5 million euros in the period 2002–05. The new company commissioned new facilities in Radovljica, and bought the robot for Seaway's expansion to enable Seaway to respond to Bavaria's demands.

Towards the end of 2001, after several months of negotiation between KD and Seaway, the brothers committed to a plan to begin producing Seaway's own sailing boats and motorboats. With finances for new technology and equipment, Seaway looked well positioned for future growth.

Further Growth

In 2001, three prestigious new clients came on board: Poncin Yachts (France), Prinz (Belgium), and AD Plastic (Croatia). Seaway started using robotic technology and, in 2002, introduced new powerboat and sailing boat models, winning its seventeenth Boat of the Year award at Boot 2002 (the world's largest international boat show) in Düsseldorf.

In 2003, Seaway teamed up with world-leading nautical designers and designed, engineered and produced the Shipman 50: the first carbon fibre sailing boat to reach series production and received prestigious awards, including the European Boat of the Year Award in 2004 (awarded at the international boat show, Boot 2004, in Düsseldorf). Seaway also designed and produced a new motorboat using carbon fibre technology. The company expanded development, and hired a manager with extensive experience in boat manufacturing and distribution. Seaway's robotics and carbon technology enabled it to begin producing products for the aviation, construction, automobile, and energy industries.

In 2004, Seaway was acknowledged by the Chamber of Industry and Commerce of Slovenia for its entrepreneurial achievements, and Jernej Jakopin for his contribution to Slovenian entrepreneurship through his management of Seaway. Seaway had become a national symbol of Slovenian success.

By 2005, Seaway achieved sales of €10 million and employed 120 people (Tables 9.4 and 9.5). By 2006, Seaway had received 22 Boat of the Year Awards, including three European Boat of the Year awards.[3]

Management Problems

In 2001, KD's investment in Seaway had been conditional upon Seaway separating the processes of design from production, and focusing resources on increasing the latter. Although the brothers agreed to the terms, it proved more difficult than expected. Japec was primarily involved in marketing and selling Seaway's boats, and conceptualizing new designs, which Jernej then developed. The brothers felt they did not have the skills and knowledge to go into large-scale production. The process of setting up and staffing a new company to manage the production soon became an area of intense conflict.

With the acquisition of the robot in 2001, new employees were hired to operate the equipment. However, a delay in building the new facilities meant that the robot could not be operationalized, and employees could not be fully utilized. The new director of the production division resigned, as did a team of designers that had been with the company since 1989. Pressure increased on the design side too, with disputes with a number of customers over licensing. As a result, Seaway ended 2001 with a loss (see Table 9.4). The partnership between KD and Seaway threatened to disintegrate.

By 2006, relations between the parties were still strained, and new areas of conflict had emerged: KD and the brothers disagreed about salaries. KD finally devised a tax-efficient proposal for securing the brothers higher guaranteed salaries, involving selling the J&J design studio brand to a third party (controlled by the Seaway group), which would then license the use of the J&J brand for €2 million over three years. This plan was, again, conditional on the brothers agreeing to begin production immediately, as KD reckoned that without large-scale production, Seaway would soon go out of business.

With a full order book that would take until 2009 to clear under the current operating structure, Seaway had stopped taking new orders, and was losing customers to competitors. KD proposed that the production company be set up in Italy (where a subsidy made the move cost-effective) under the management of an Austrian company with extensive production experience, with whom KD signed an agreement-in-principle. The separate production company would enable Seaway to grow very fast, allowing the brothers to continue to focus on design. To expedite the process, KD put in place a new management team, and brought on board an experienced production management consultant. The new team developed a production forecast and income projections (the first such reports to be generated in the Seaway group) which confirmed that increased production and profits were highly realistic and achievable.

KD also suggested that a new board of directors be hired to manage the production company, with Japec as chairman. Toward the end of 2006, it appeared as if the brothers would agree to KD's plan, and allow the new company to be set up and begin production.

UNDERSTANDING ENTREPRENEURIAL ACTIVITY

As mentioned previously, the approach suggested by Shane and Venkataraman (2000) enables us to analyse the personal and environmental factors that contributed to the development and success of Seaway.

Entrepreneurs form firms to create wealth, but the manner in which this occurs depends on the environmental context (Ireland et al. 2001). Baker et al. (2005) elaborate on the ways in which entrepreneurial activity is context-dependent, using the model of Shane and Venkataraman (2000). They argue that a nation's social context, including its institutions and culture, strongly affects both the available opportunities and the individuals who discover and exploit them (Figure 9.1).

Shane and Venkataraman (2000) suggest that the discovery of opportunities is based on access to information (determined by past experience and specialized information), and cognitive properties (determined by individual abilities). Baker et al. (2005) note that these factors are context-specific. In particular they argue that discovery is most likely dominated by advantaged individuals with access to knowledge and social networks, a description that clearly characterized the Jakopins.[4]

The evaluation of opportunities refers to the calculation of expected returns. Here the issue is why different people might evaluate the same

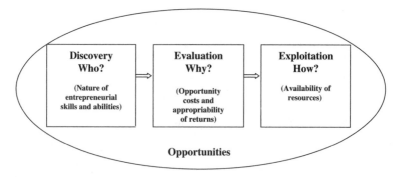

Source: Adapted from Baker et al. (2005).

Figure 9.1   Understanding the entrepreneurial process

opportunity differently, and this in turn depends on both opportunity costs and the ability to appropriate rewards. Baker et al. (2005) argue that opportunity costs and appropriability regimes vary across national contexts. For example, differences in unemployment rates and wages across countries create differences in opportunity costs, while differences in legal regimes and protection of property rights create differences in appropriation possibilities.

Finally, the exploitation of opportunities depends on access to critical resources including finance and human capital. Baker et al. (2005) distinguish between access to specialized and complementary assets, which are often provided through regional agglomerations (clusters) and generic infrastructure, which is available (if at all) regardless of location. They do not, however, discuss the importance of access to foreign resources, a factor emphasized in Aidis (2005) who points to the potential benefits (and threats) to small economies arising from EU membership. While the net benefits are not always unambiguous, it is likely that they are stronger for small countries, whose domestic markets are not sufficiently large to sustain firms of efficient size. Thus, companies in small countries such as Slovenia may benefit from access to a large market, although they may also face increased competition at home.

THE ENVIRONMENT FOR ENTREPRENEURSHIP IN SLOVENIA

In this section, we analyse the Slovenian environment in terms of the general discovery, evaluation and exploitation framework. We will discuss how these three elements were affected by the particular characteristics of Slovenia as a transition economy. We also discuss how market failures, a common characteristic of transition economies (McMillan and Woodruff 2002), manifested themselves in Slovenia.

The Discovery of Opportunities[5]

According to Shane and Venkataraman (2000), the discovery of opportunities is based on access to information and cognitive properties, and discovery is dominated by advantaged individuals with access to knowledge and social networks. Slovenia was relatively highly industrialized and fairly well integrated into the world economy. There were a large number of professionals who perceived the opportunities arising from the lack of supply of products and services which can best be served by smaller enterprises. In the initial years of transition in the 1990s there was therefore a surge in the creation of new firms, particularly in businesses which did not require major financial and physical resources. The social strata of people who perceived and exploited these opportunities were mainly managers and engineers and staff in former state-owned enterprises, people with business experience and established social networks (Aidis 2005). In addition, there were a relatively small number of professional entrepreneurs (in the sense of Peng and Shekshinia 2001) who found opportunities in businesses not necessarily related to their professional experiences. Peng and Shekshnia (2001) refer to professional entrepreneurs as those who previously had a profession that was not related to the ruling party.

It should be noted that opportunities in the SME sector were relatively more attractive because the option of taking over and restructuring existing enterprises was made difficult by the Slovenian privatization model, which did not permit management buy-out/ins. This option was rejected in favour of voucher privatization, which led to the creation of opportunities for a special group of entrepreneurs who set up privatization funds which allowed them to acquire significant financial wealth through generous management fees. The owners of privatization funds possessed important investment capabilities, and were instrumental in the development of the mutual funds and venture capital industries, and the working of the Ljubljana stock exchange. Stock market capitalization as a percentage of GDP continues to grow, but it is still only slightly above average relative to other transition economies (Table 9.2).[6] However, Slovenia ranks above the average in terms of investor protection and disclosure, according to the World Bank (2006). Thus, relatively active financial markets represent important factors contributing to the exploitation of opportunities.

The Evaluation of Opportunities

The evaluation of opportunities refers to the calculation of expected returns, which in turn depends on opportunity costs and the ability to appropriate rewards. As in other transition economies, in Slovenia many people with skills lost their jobs or were working in companies which struggled for survival so that the opportunity cost of setting up a company was very low. In general, low opportunity costs are common in transition markets, and as a result, most new enterprises are needs-based rather than opportunity-driven (Smallbone and Welter 2001).[7]

Also, in the early 1990s the regime for setting up companies was very liberal.[8] A number of incentives were introduced, including reduced profit taxes in the initial years, subsidies for starting up companies and employing workers, and a reinvestment tax credit, all of which contributed to the reduction of opportunity costs. Profit appropriability was encouraged by the absence of a capital gains tax (until 2000), lax accounting standards and favourable bankruptcy procedures which favoured debtors not creditors.

Thus, in general the opportunity cost was relatively low and the ability to appropriate returns relatively high. This resulted in a high rate of new firm creation, particularly micro enterprises with minimal financial and physical resource requirements. On the other hand, in the area of high-tech industries and industries with higher resource availability there was no significant new firm creation and the same was true of enterprise restructuring.[9]

The Exploitation of Opportunities

Exploitation of opportunities depends on access to critical resources, including physical assets, human capital and finance. There were two limiting factors preventing the entry of firms with higher financial and physical requirements in Slovenia. First, real interest rates were very high in the transition period (up to 30 per cent). Second, in spite of a large number of bankruptcies, commercial land and physical assets were not available for use by new entrepreneurial ventures. The reason for this was that companies borrowing at high interest rates to finance working capital were securing the loans by mortgaging land and plants mostly at book value which was well above market value. The banks then carried these assets on their balance sheets and refused to write off the value of these assets in order to prevent their own bankruptcies. In addition, the bankruptcy procedures were legally structured in such a way that they allowed protracted proceedings which enabled bankruptcy managers to hold high prices of land and assets for a long time. In the initial transition years new businesses were limited in growth by these two factors. Most of the growth of SMEs was therefore in businesses that did not require high financial resources and/or physical assets.

In addition to these difficulties there was a problem in the 1990s with access to specialized and skilled human capital. In particular, high-tech companies found human resources an important constraint. These constraints were caused by shortages and labour market rigidities that made hiring difficult.[10] In particular, the tax and social security system made the hiring of well-paid people very expensive for small firms. For example, a progressive payroll tax introduced in the 1990s put high-tech companies at a competitive disadvantage, because it increased labour costs to the company for high-wage workers. This problem was exacerbated by the fact that many such companies increasingly required skilled foreign workers, whose salaries were driven up by the payroll tax. Tax reform is now under way and has produced some relief through gradual elimination of the payroll tax, and reduction in personal income tax (from 50 per cent to 41 per cent at the highest rate).

Although it was not so in the early transition years, due to global competition and prudent public finance, financial markets have become more competitive and finance is now available at competitive international rates to all enterprises. Formal and informal venture capital is becoming increasingly available due to the high liquidity of Slovenian households. Public policy encourages entrepreneurship with a support infrastructure including subsidized business advice which is available throughout Slovenia. In addition, the Slovenian government has attempted to establish a cluster infrastructure which is helping to reduce the problem of specialized resources and complementary assets. Throughout Slovenia, incubators, technological parks and industrial zones are rapidly developing, easing the problem of availability of suitable physical facilities.[11]

Nevertheless, internal analysis by Seaway, evaluating the relative advantage of industrial locations in Slovenia and Italy clearly shows that locations in Italy, in which just under 40 per cent of the world's luxury yachts are designed and built, and in which major industrial centres for boatbuilding have developed, are advantageous. Thus, the Slovenian environment still poses a major problem for entrepreneurial development.[12]

THE BROTHERS JAPEC AND JERNEJ JAKOPIN

The personal background of the Jakopin brothers is essential in understanding their emergence as entrepreneurs, and in particular their ability to discover, evaluate and exploit opportunities. Japec and Jernej Jakopin were born into a high-profile and highly regarded family in Ljubljana, Slovenia's capital city. Their mother was a renowned writer, who had married an acclaimed academic – a member of the prestigious Slovenian Academy of Science and Arts – in the field of Slavic languages.

Both sons were expected to be excellent students of maths and the classics, and respected careers were assigned at early ages. Japec studied medicine, achieved straight As and, in 1976, at age 26, was the youngest medical student to complete his PhD. By the age of 29 he was a well-known cardiology researcher. Jernej became an architect. He left immediately after his studies to set up his own company in Germany, which became highly successful.

The brothers were therefore in many respects well suited to the process of discovery of opportunities. They were well-educated, one of them had foreign experience and contacts, and they came from an advantaged background. However, as professionals and academics, they were outside the ruling networks of the day. This may have been an advantage, because it limited their entrepreneurial focus to new ventures, as opposed to existing ones that were more closely linked to the political elite.

Both were skilled recreational sailors, with extensive knowledge of the latest technological and engineering techniques. In 1983, Japec brazenly contacted the chief executive of Elan, a local boat-building company that had expanded from its origins as the world leader in ski manufacturing, to inform him that his choice of Swedish boat designers was a poor one. Japec was invited to replace the Swedish designers, an offer which he accepted. However, never having built a boat by himself, Japec called Jernej in Germany for assistance. Jernej returned to Slovenia.

The brothers immediately asked the advice of Olympic sailors. The racers did not know about boat-building, but they had intimate knowledge of what they needed from a boat in order to win a race. Approaching boat-building from the 'lead' users' perspective was unprecedented at the time even outside of Slovenia, but together the brothers and racers collaborated to determine the characteristics of a really great boat.

The Jakopins bought rudimentary software to assist them with the boat design. The completed design was built in Elan's manufacturing facilities, and the finished boat, named Elan 31, was taken to Sweden to be raced competitively. The boat won the regatta, and repeatedly proved itself unbeatable in its class.

The Jakopins achieved instant fame for their award-winning boat, and Elan asked them to continue to supply it with designs. The brothers agreed and Japec, then 33, resigned his position as a cardiology researcher, and Jernej (at age 26) abandoned his career in Germany and moved back to Slovenia. For tax purposes, they set up a new partnership called J&J design studio, through which Japec would manage Elan's boat building division, which would build boats designed by Jernej.

Between 1983 and 1987, the brothers designed ten sailing boats (eight for Elan) and travelled all over Europe selling them. In 1985, the Elan 31 won the world series three-quarter ton yacht championship in Sweden. Elan's exports of nautical products grew from 2 million DM to 20 million DM (€1 to 10 million) during this period.

In 1987, Elan came under new management and decided to refocus its strategy on making skis. Premier French boat-building company, Jeanneau, had been tracking Elan's success, and invited Japec to lead its marketing division in La Rochelle, France. Jernej stayed in Slovenia and took over control of J&J design company. Between 1987 and 1990, with the help of the latest technology (their villa in Ljubljana was the first in Yugoslavia to have a dedicated telephone line for the facsimile transmission of blueprints) the brothers designed eight boats for Jeanneau. Jeanneau's sales grew from 514m to 840m FF (€78 to 128 million), with significant contribution by the

Sun Odyssey sailboat range designed by J&J design studio. These events led to the founding of Seaway in 1989, as discussed above.

It is clear from this history that the Jakopin brothers fit neatly into the 'professional entrepreneur' category (Peng and Shekshnia 2001), comprising people who had a profession not related to the ruling party. Professional entrepreneurs are more likely to form technology-based companies, and to engage in prospecting, meaning that they are likely to choose activities based on innovation, flexibility and market orientation. The emphasis on lead users is an important example, and one that was typically ignored in transition economies where the legacy of production-led thinking often prevailed.

Consistent with previous evidence (Roberts and Zhou 2000), the brothers were professionals seeking a career change. However, neither of them was unemployed or working in a firm with uncertain prospects, nor had they been engaged in previous illegal activities, as has been found in other transition markets (Earle and Sakova 2000). In this respect their opportunity costs were high, and not low. This, combined with their high levels of education, results in an evaluation of opportunities that favours entry into high-technology and knowledge-based activities (Smallbone and Welter 2001). At the same time, small knowledge-based firms are in a better position to appropriate profits if their skills cannot easily be imitated. Such was clearly the case for their design capabilities.

In terms of exploitation, it seems clear that the brothers were able to be successful so long as the company remained small and focused on design. Under these circumstances few employees were needed, sophisticated managerial skills were not necessary, and capital requirements were low. However, when it became necessary for the company to become larger, the resource constraints became binding and the brothers were forced to seek outside financing.

SEAWAY: PROSPECTS

With the infusion of new capital by KD in 2000/2001 the company performance improved. Growth has been accompanied by increased profitability (tables 9.4 and 9.5). A recent assessment put Seaway's value at more than triple what it had been in 2001, driven largely by demand in Eastern Europe, facilitated by the expansion of the European Union. Going forward, however, a focus on the production process is required in order to maintain the pace of technological development, and to accelerate growth.

But the expansion has diluted the control of the Jakopin brothers, and led to pressures to install professional management. There is now in place a supervisory board with a majority formed by KD or external members.

Therefore, despite the aggressive growth strategy, the company may be unable to achieve its targets given the tension between the brothers and the board. Much will depend on the company's ability to build a more structured, profit-driven enterprise on Seaway's innovative roots.

SEAWAY: SUMMARY AND CONCLUSIONS

Seaway is a well-publicized success story in Slovenia. Its features include strong founders with entrepreneurial capabilities who succeeded despite the relative hostility of the business environment. The company was developed by people whose qualifications were not in sailing or boats; a world-class company was developed out of a hobby. However, its success was based on innovative design and new technologies. Venture capital investment was critical, allowing the Jakopin brothers to produce their own boats and so to diversify from design to production. At the same time, this has diluted their control, and led to pressures to install professional management.

In many ways, the Seaway story is generic, and resembles the story of many entrepreneurial companies in many environments. As documented by Markides and Geroski (2005) it is not unusual, and may be optimal, for small innovative firms to lose their independence as the importance of routinized management increases. At the same time, the company did emerge from an environment which was (and is) to some degree hostile to entrepreneurship, and where many others failed, or failed to emerge. The case clearly identifies the critical importance of venture capital and financial markets in this process of growth.

The case also sheds light on the emerging academic literature on international entrepreneurship. For the most part, the Seaway story can be understood using the discovery, evaluation, exploitation framework at both the levels of the firm and its founders, as well as at the level of the country. This provides a greater understanding of the ways in which the specific institutional environment affected the emergence and success of this company. In this case, it appears that the relatively liberal environment in the former Yugoslavia fostered an environment in which highly-educated people could remain outside the political establishment, and even maintain foreign contacts. The evidence suggests that these are the precisely the people who are most likely to overcome barriers to entrepreneurship.

ACKNOWLEDGEMENTS

We are grateful to Mari Nurminen for her excellent research assistance.

NOTES

1. 'Družba z omejeno odgovornostjo', meaning a company with limited liability.
2. This is consistent with the evidence in Bukvic and Bartlett (2003) indicating that the main financial barriers for SME growth in Slovenia were high cost of capital, high collateral requirements for loans, banks' bureaucratic procedures, and banks' lack of interest (Table 2, p. 165).
3. A complete list of awards obtained by the company can be found at: http://www.seaway.si.
4. They also note, paradoxically, that exclusion from social networks may lead to the creation or exploitation of alternatives, as is the case with ethnic minorities in various countries.
5. The following sections are based on Vahčič and Petrin (1990) and d'Andrea Tyson et al. (1994).
6. Bygrave and Hunt (2005) report in their Global Entrepreneurship Monitor (GEM) study that of countries surveyed in 2003, Slovenia ranks last in terms of venture capital as a percentage of GDP. However, none of the other countries surveyed were transition economies. However, Mueller and Goic (2002), in comparing entrepreneurial potential among transition economies rank Slovenia second.
7. In addition, evidence from GEM (Bygrave and Hunt 2005) suggests that 'necessity' is the main driving source for entrepreneurial activity in emerging and transition markets.
8. Nevertheless, today the time required to start a business in Slovenia is above that of other transition economies (Table 9.2).
9. However, Damaskopoulos and Evgeniou (2003) report that of four East European countries studied (Slovenia, Romania, Poland and Bulgaria) Slovenia is the most advanced in terms of adaptation of e-business.
10. According to the World Bank, Slovenia is still below the average of transition economies in terms of difficulty in hiring and labour market rigidity (World Bank 2006). The Economist Intelligence Unit (2006) describes labour markets as 'relatively inflexible'.
11. There is some debate regarding the success of clustering initiatives. Drnovsek and Kovacic (2003) suggest that even though Slovenia has been one of the more successful transition economies, its relative competitiveness position has not improved compared to some other transition countries despite the clustering policy.
12. Interview with Professor Ales Vahcic, head of Entrepreneurship in the department of Economics, University of Llubljana, on 19 September 2006.

REFERENCES

Aidis, R. (2005), 'Entrepreneurship in Transition Countries: A Review', Working Paper No. 61, Centre for the Study of Economic and Social Change in Europe, London: UCL School of Slavonic and East European Studies.

Baker, T., E. Gedajlovic and M. Lubatkin (2005), 'A Framework for Comparing Entrepreneurship Processes across Countries', *Journal of International Business Studies*, **36**, 492–504.

Bygrave, W. and S. Hunt (2005), *Global Entrepreneurship Monitor 2004 Financing Report*, Babson College and London Business School.

Bukvic, V. and W. Bartlett (2003), 'Financial Barriers to SME Growth in Slovenia', *Economic and Business Review for Central and South-Eastern Europe*, Oct (5), 161–81.

Damaskopoulos, P. and T. Evgeniou (2003), 'Adoption of New Economy Practices by SMEs in Eastern Europe', *European Management Journal*, **21**, 133–45.

D'Andrea Tyson, L., T. Petrin and H. Rogers (1994), 'Promoting Entrepreneurship in Eastern Europe', *Small Business Economics*, **6** (3), 165–84.

Drnovsek, M. and A. Kovacic (2003), 'Why Slovenia Lags in International Competitiveness Development: A Framework for Analyzing a Competitive Environment for Clustering', *Economic and Business Review*, **5**, 183–200.

Earle, J. and Z. Sakova (2000), 'Business Start-Ups or Disguised Unemployment? Evidence on the Character of Self-Employment from Transition Economies', *Labour Economics*, **7**, 575–601.

Economist Intelligence Unit (2006), *Slovenia Country Profile*, London.

European Bank of Reconstruction and Development (EBRD) (2005), *Transition Report: Business in Transition*, London: EBRD.

European Commission (2005), '2005 European Innovation Scoreboard', http://www.trendchart.org/scoreboards/scoreboard2005/docs/EIS2005_database.xls, accessed 21 June 2006.

European Innovation Scoreboard (2005), *European Trend Chart on Innovation*, http://www.trendchart.org, accessed 17 September 2006.

Ireland, R. Duane, Michael Hitt, S. Michael Camp and Donald L. Sexton (2001), 'Integrating Entrepreneurship and Strategic Management Actions to Create Firm Wealth', *Academy of Management Executive*, **15** (1), 49–63.

Khanna, T. and J. Rivkin (2001), 'Estimating the Performance Effects of Business Groups in Emerging Markets', *Strategic Management Journal*, Jan (22), 45–74.

Khanna, T., Krishna G. Palepu and Jayant Sinha (2005), 'Strategies that Fit Emerging Markets', *Harvard Business Review*, June, 63–73.

Markides, C. and P. Geroski (2005), *Fast Second*, San Francisco: Jossey-Bass.

McMillan, J. and C. Woodruff (2002), 'The Central Role of Entrepreneurs in Transition Economies', *Journal of Economic Perspectives*, Summer (16), 153–70.

Meyer, K. and M. Peng (2005), 'Probing Theoretically into Central and Eastern Europe: Transactions, Resources, and Institutions', *Journal of International Business Studies*, **36**, 600–621.

Mueller, S. and S. Goic (2002), 'Entrepreneurial Potential in Transition Economies: A View from Tomorrow's Leaders', *Journal of Developmental Entrepreneurship*, Dec (7), 399–414.

Peng, M. and S. Shekshnia (2001), 'How Entrepreneurs Create Wealth in Transition Economies', *The Academy of Management Executive*, Feb (15), 95.

Roberts, K. and C. Zhou (2000), 'New Private Enterprises in Three Transitional Contexts: Central Europe, the Former Soviet Union and China', *Post-Communist Economies*, **12**, 186–99.

Shane, S. and S. Venkataraman (2000), 'The Promise of Entrepreneurship as a Field of Research', *Academy of Management Review*, **25** (1), 217–26.

Smallbone, D. and F. Welter (2001), 'The Distinctiveness of Entrepreneurship in Transition Economies', *Small Business Economics*, **16**, 249–62.

Vahčič, A. and T. Petrin (1990), 'Restructuring the Yugoslav Economy through the Development of Entrepreneurship, and the Role of the Financial System', *Society for Slovenian Studies: Slovenian Studies*, **12** (1), 67–73.

World Bank (2006), 'Doing Business Indicators 2006', http://www.doingbusiness.org, accessed 21 June 2006.

Index